MW01169752

Florida
Men

A Road Atlas
for Single Women

Felicia Michele Haber

SHOT TOWER BOOKS
Boca Raton, Florida

Printed in the United States of America

Senior Editor: Judith Strauss
Managing Editor: Katie Yeakle
Production Editor: Kimberlee Lansdale
Illustrator: Rick Tulka
Cover Designer: Jean Cohn

Published by:
    Shot Tower Books, Inc.
    150 East Palmetto Park Road
    Suite 320
    Boca Raton, Florida 33432

ISBN 0-9639629-5-7 softcover

Distributed in the book trade by Atrium Publishers Group

This book is dedicated to my two best friends and favorite Florida women — my mother, Eva Rosen and my sister, Tania Nicole Haber. Thanks for your endless supply of love, humor, and encouragement. Also dedicated in memory of my grandmother, Sonia Zak Efron.

Special thanks to:

*Catherine-Anne Hovenden
Mark Ford
Kelley Comiskey
Barbara Perriello
Courtney Rubin
Larry Sarner
Ramala Basu
Carmen Campbell
Tom Spalding
Nancy Klingener
Elinor Brecher*

Table of Contents

Introduction vii

Chapter 1: The Male Animal 1
Chapter 2: True Stories, Part I 51
Chapter 3: Where the Boys Are 59
Chapter 4: True Stories, Part II 71
Chapter 5: Playing the Numbers Game 77
Chapter 6: Meeting Strategies and Dating Tips 83
Chapter 7: True Stories, Part III 93
Chapter 8: Alternative Ways to Meet Men 97
Chapter 9: True Stories, Part IV 109
Chapter 10: What Every Single Woman Should Know .. 117
Chapter 11: The Best Places to Find Florida Men 125

Appendix: Singles/Networking Groups 181

Bibliography 195

About the Author 197

Introduction

Finding a man in Florida is like finding a parking space at the mall during a big sale. You have to be either very lucky or willing to fight.

Some women blame the problem on the humidity. They feel anything that can have such a negative effect on their hair can be blamed for just about anything. Others think it must have something to do with the damaging effects of the sun — that the pool of eligible men somehow evaporated.

The truth is, there are plenty of great men here. And contrary to popular belief, the median age of Florida men is not dead. That's just a rumor started years ago by Florida women who wanted to discourage the competition. The majority of our men really do mean cars when they say "wheels" — not chairs.

But it is just a little harder to meet men in Florida. For one thing, our cities are so spread out. The only men you're likely to see every day work in your office or at a toll plaza. You're also unlikely to meet men on a bus or train, because hardly anyone uses public transportation.

The state's lack of intellectually demanding industry doesn't help either. Citrus and tourism don't exactly attract a bountiful supply of men with commitment on their minds. And because Florida is so transient, it's not uncommon to fall in love with someone who ends up moving back home or to a better job in another state. These factors combine to make Florida a tough place for dating.

Tough, not *impossible*. Just because it's harder to get a date here doesn't mean you won't. Think of it this way: How many people does it take to make a match? Two. And since you're one of them, you're already halfway there. That's right, you're only one person away from a date! Why, then, is it that with thousands of eligible men in Florida, the only one you see on Saturday night is delivering your pizza?

Maybe, just maybe, the problem is you. Maybe your energies are misdirected. Be honest with yourself. Do you spend your free time on the phone male-bashing with your girlfriends? Sitting on the couch watching "Men Are Deplorable Creatures and There's Nothing You Can Do About It" on *Geraldo*? Reading "Why Men Are Pigs" in the latest issue of *Cosmo*?

Well, it's time to hang up the phone, get off the couch, and put down the pathetic magazine articles. Good things don't happen to people who sit around and wait for them, they happen to people who get up and look for them. That's how you found your apartment, your car, and your job, isn't it?

You just have to know where to go to meet men. You also have to know what to do and what to say when you meet them. That's where we come in. Think of this book as your personal guide through Florida's dating zoo.

And, boy, is Florida an exciting place to explore! Where else can you be picked up by a Jewish guy on a Harley who takes you out for dinner at a Cuban restaurant, a visit to a Haitian art museum, and late-night dancing at a country western bar? Certainly not in Minnesota.

Chapter 1

The Male Animal

*The 24 Most Common Species
in the Florida Dating Zoo*

If Florida were a giant zoo (and some people think it is), it would have the world's most extensive collection of male species — some in larger herds than others.

As in any dating jungle, the strongest and most powerful males are most sought after for mating, and the weakest most often chewed up and spit out.

Here, then, in no particular order, are two dozen of the most common of the Florida male "species" to be on the lookout for. Decide for yourself which ones you want to go after — and which ones would be better left in cages.

Jacked-Up Jack *(hickus redneckus)*

Jacked-Up Jack is unique because he is a true native of the state. His primary mode of transportation is a confederate-flag-waving-jacked-up-used-Ford-pick-up-truck. If he doesn't pick you up in it, that's because his cousins are in town and need a place to bed down for the night. When he's away from his truck, you can identify him by his "Kiss My Bass" T-shirt, the Skoal tin peeking out of the back pocket on his Wrangler-wrapped buttocks, and the several blurry tattoos that not even he can decipher.

He can be a great date, as long as you catch him on payday, soon after a quick stop at his personal financial institution, The Check Cashing Store.

A typical night on the town with Jacked-Up Jack might include alligator wrestling or monster truck madness (his favorite spectator sports), followed by a visit to his favorite restaurant — Bud's All-You-Can-Eat Open Pit BBQ.

This predator generally mates very close to home. (More than a few Jacked-Up Jacks meet their soulmates at family reunions.)

Florida's Jacked-Up Jack
(hickus redneckus)

Man-a-Tee Mel *(stomachus bulgus)*

Named after the Florida mammal — though not, himself, an endangered species — Man-a-Tee Mel likes to play up his striking physical resemblance to his namesake by sporting worn T-shirts that end just above his large, sack-like stomach.

If you date a Man-a-Tee Mel, you can be sure he'll be faithful — he simply doesn't have the energy to fool around. He is a stationary species, rarely lifting himself from his recliner. When he does get up, you'll find him roaming the aisles of the local food wholesale warehouse, stocking up on bulk quantities of Bud and chips. And on weekends, you'll find him outfitting himself at the nearest flea market or yard sale.

Florida's Man-a-Tee Mel
(stomachus bulgus)

Copper Tony *(askinfora melanoma)*

Tony did not inherit his shiny, leathery coat from his ancestors. He got it the hard way — by spending countless hours dedicated to basking in the sun's rays. With any luck, you'll meet a member of this species capable of funneling some of this same devotion into a relationship.

You'll meet Copper Tony on the beach (of course), where he spends his days moving in circles, like the hands on a clock, readjusting himself to catch the strongest rays. If Copper Tony is the man for you, you can look forward to romantic evenings snuggling on the couch while watching the Weather Channel's tan index — and to exciting excursions when it's raining, searching, together, for a beach where it isn't.

Florida's Copper Tony
(askinfora melanoma)

Pumped-Up Jim *(musclus grandus)*

Jim's gym is his natural habitat, from which he rarely emerges. It doesn't matter what time it is — 7 a.m., 3 p.m., midnight — he'd rather work out than work.

You'll run into him at the water fountain on your way to aerobics. If you like the way he fills out his muscle shirt, and admire his choice of a weight belt as a fashion accessory, Pumped-Up Jim may be your Mr. Right.

A relationship with Pumped-Up Jim will get started when he asks you to drop by the weight room and "spot" him after your class. (If you think this means he wants you to stare at him, you're only half right.) Things will heat up when he offers to help you do a little body sculpting — and you'll know things are really getting serious if he invites you up to his place for a power shake.

Florida's Pumped-Up Jim
(musclus grandus)

Gameboy Gary *(sportus addictus)*

His natural habitat is anywhere there's a ball and a flock of jocks. Indoors or out, Gameboy Garys find each other by tuning into the phrase, "Hey man, do you know the score?"

In an advanced stage of addiction, a Gameboy Gary lives and breathes "The Game." Get too close to him, and he's likely to bellow, "Time out." His memory is quite amazing. He can keep track of all the scores of games going on in front of him, on his pocket television, on his radio, and on the listening devices carried by nearby Gameboy Garys. Unfortunately, he cannot remember his own address or your telephone number without writing it down.

Florida's Gameboy Gary
(sportus addictus)

Nine-Hole Norm *(hole-in-oneus is-my-dreamus)*

Nine-Hole Norm's life begins and ends on the golf course, and all his business deals are wrapped up at the 19th hole.

If you meet a member of this species that has only a mild addiction to golf, think of it as a positive. A relationship with him will leave you plenty of time for an occasional afternoon of recreational shopping, or a fun outing with "the girls."

However, stay away from him if he has an extreme case of this addiction. If he concentrates too much on his golf game, he won't be able to concentrate on you.

Florida's Nine-Hole Norm
(hole-in-oneus is-my-dreamus)

Earlybird Ernie *(drivingus off-the-roadus)*

Earlybird Ernie is a very diversified — and productive — guy. He is quite capable of playing a round of golf, making two doctor appointments, reading the paper from front to back, causing six traffic jams, walking four miles, cross-checking every sale item at three different grocery stores, and playing a game of cards — all before 10 a.m.!

Earlybird Ernies thrive on a strict low-salt, low-fat, low-sugar diet of "Early Bird" dinners and prune juice, and their motto is, "Early to bed, and early to rise" — but maybe just a little too early for you. If he is a widower, he is one of the most sought-after creatures in his condo.

Florida's Earlybird Ernie
(drivingus off-the-roadus)

Mid-Life Mitch *(crisis convertiblus)*

Mid-Life Mitch is not exactly a separate species. He's really just an ordinary guy who suddenly hits his 40th birthday.

At that moment in time, he undergoes a frightening metamorphosis, shedding his sensible Oldsmobile in favor of anything convertible. He watches MTV for hours on end, and practices saying "cool!" in front of the mirror. His motto becomes, "Plugs, Not Drugs," and he grows out whatever hair he has so he can either wear it in a ponytail (subspecies "Baldy Locks"), or wrap it across the top of his head.

A voice inside him tells him to hunt younger prey — long-legged blondes who will reinforce his new self-image. Or at least agree to be seen with him.

Fortunately, this is almost never a permanent condition. Once Mid-Life Mitch gets through this unstable period, he *will* mellow out.

Florida's Mid-Life Mitch
(crisis convertiblus)

Harley Hank *(bikeus orbustus)*

This attention-seeker on the prowl most often travels in packs in South Beach and Daytona Beach, and on major Florida highways.

His distinguishing features are a black helmet (also used for beer storage), black T-shirt, black leather pants or blue jeans well-worn in just the right spots, and black leather boots with plenty of chrome trim. He signals he is ready to mate by lifting his helmet and shaking his head vigorously.

Don't get jealous if he brags about his "girl" — he's only talking about his bike.

Florida's Harley Hank
(bikeus orbustus)

Surfin Scooter *(wavus nonexistus)*

One of the best built and leanest of all the species, Surfin Scooters are very popular with young Florida females.

This barefoot bleach-blond predator dude with golden cheeks and a dazzling white smile has a spectacular collection of jazzy Jams that can be spotted several nautical miles away.

You'll find him pacing up and down the shore, searching for the perfect wave — or at least anything over three feet. Hurricane season is his favorite time of year, and Melbourne, Sebastian Inlet, and Panama City are some of his favorite haunts.

If you date a Surfin Scooter, be sure you specify exactly what you mean by "Wear a suit" when you invite him to your holiday office party.

Florida's Surfin Scooter
(wavus nonexistus)

Margaritaville Mick *(loafus aroundus)*
   Margaritaville Mick is the most laid-back of all the species. He is found predominantly in Key West with his shirt unevenly buttoned and a 5-day beard. This flip-flop-shod specimen feeds on rum runners and conch, and decorates his habitat solely with lobster traps and stuffed fish.

   If you wonder why he doesn't make a pass at you, it's because he's probably passed out. He does everything at a leisurely pace. He doesn't drink, he *sips*. He doesn't walk, he *ambles*. He doesn't swim, he *floats*. The most strenuous exercise he gets is when his eyes glaze over at the sight of a sunset or the sound of a Jimmy Buffett tune.

   If you want to turn him on, whisper his favorite Spanish word into his ear — "mañana." And if your name happens to be Margarita, you're set!

Florida's Margaritaville Mick
(loafus aroundus)

Barney Cal *(myboatus is-my-lifeus)*

Though you will find Barney Cals in the same general vicinity as Surfin Scooters and Margaritaville Micks, they are a very, very different breed. They are really much closer in temperament to another one of the highly obsessed species — Gameboy Garys. But Barney Cals are just as obsessed with the gear as they are with the game. Every Barney Cal's main goal in life is to outwit the fish, and outfish everyone else on the water.

If you date a Barney Cal, you'll never have to worry about losing track of him — he's always anchored to his boat. If you're lucky, you may catch him in the pre-dawn hours, just before he shoves off. If you miss him then, you'll have to wait until he rolls back in with the tide, one foot planted triumphantly atop a huge cooler full of his catch of the day.

Florida's Barney Cal
(myboatus is-my-lifeus)

Vanity Vince *(egotistus grandus)*

Vanity Vinces are the fastest growing, and most decorative, of the species. They are almost always actor/models, and are found primarily in South Beach and Orlando living on imported bottled water, leafy greens, and iced cappuccino.

Vanity Vinces spend much of their time on Rollerblades, searching for their own reflections in store windows, rear view mirrors, and rain puddles. When they feel the need to seek out a mate, they don't discriminate — they'll take a man or a woman.

Vanity Vinces make eye-catching accessories, but you might prefer a species that attracts less attention than you do.

Florida's Vanity Vince
(egotistus grandus)

Tourist Tom *(wifeus back-in-the-roomus)*

This predator can be easily identified by his permanent smile, his scarlet complexion, the white line on his ring finger, and his boundless energy.

After a full day cheering on trained seals and zipping down water slides, he leaves the wife and kids at the hotel and slips out for a little adult entertainment.

Tourist Tom is a hit with some Florida women because he has an endless supply of traveler's checks that he loves to spend on them. But don't get carried away by his generosity. A relationship with this species will last only as long as his vacation.

Florida's Tourist Tom
(wifeus back-in-the-roomus)

Mako Mario *(tawkstoomuchus aboutnewyawkus)*

Mako Mario lurks in dark after-hours singles bars. He is always on the make — so aggressively that some women mistake him for Andrew Dice Clay. He emigrated from New York (though no one can figure out why), and is convinced that any reference to "The City" works as an instant aphrodisiac.

You'll know a Mako Mario finds you extremely attractive if he sidles up to you and begins to make loud comments about Joey and the boys from the block, Howard Stern, and his perfect Ma up on Lawng Island.

Florida's Mako Mario
(tawkstoomuchus aboutnewyawkus)

Cellular Sal *(beepus faxus)*

Cellular Sal is a lone wolf whose idea of a mating call is to call you from his car — when he's a block from your house. He avoids being around his own kind, because he gets so confused when someone else's phone is ringing. (If you want to impress him, tell him you'd recognize the sound of his beep anywhere.)

The only problem with Cellular Sal is that he doesn't age well. Years of dependence on little devices hooked to his belt eventually erode his in-person skills. You know he's reached this stage when he says, "I'm turned on" — but is simply referring to the fact that his phone is working.

Florida's Cellular Sal
(beepus faxus)

Rico Suave *(donjuanus syndromus)*

There are more Latin lovers in Miami than there are in South America, Central America, and the Caribbean combined. And it's easy to see why women find them so attractive. Rico Suave is the smoothest, most romantic, and best-smelling of the male species. Unfortunately, he is also the most possessive.

He loves all of Florida's "chicas." His eyes wander from backside to backside, all the while with a firm grip on yours. Don't worry if you don't speak Spanish. The only word he wants to hear you say is "si."

Florida's Rico Suave
(donjuanus syndromus)

Hurricane Andrew *(ontherunus from-some-where-elseus)*

Named Hurricane Andrew because he is the Florida woman's own natural disaster, this species is known for coming on strong and leaving a trail of devastation.

He is one of the most dangerous of the common species because he is so unpredictable. He is also one of the most wanted — wanted in six states by tax collectors, ex-wives, the police, etc. His habitat is a $35-a-week motel room furnished with one suitcase that's always packed and ready for a quick getaway.

Be suspicious that you may be dating a Hurricane Andrew if he always pays in cash, doesn't have a phone — and especially if you keep running into people who know him by another name.

Florida's Hurricane Andrew
(ontherunus from-somewhere-elseus)

Tipme Todd *(pockets full-of-pleasurus)*

Tipme Todd is one of the most charming and resourceful of the male species. His smile alone lures many unsuspecting females into his den. But beware — his life support depends on tips. That smooth line he gave you last night is one he'll be giving someone else tonight.

Tipme Todds flourish in central Florida, the state's tourist mecca, where their service-oriented skills — mixing drinks, parking cars, and giving directions — are in greatest demand.

Erratic creatures because their work is so unpredictable, Tipme Todds will wine and dine you while the cash is flowing, but forget your name when tourist season ends. And don't be fooled by those huge wads of cash they carry — they're all one-dollar bills.

A Tipme Todd may be an entertaining date, but if you're looking for stability, look elsewhere.

Florida's Tipme Todd
(pockets full-of-pleasurus)

Snakey Sam *(swampsalesmanus amongus)*

Snakey Sam (short for "scam") isn't looking for a date, he's looking for a deal. He'll tell you anything he thinks you want to hear in order to get you to sign on the dotted line. Recent widows and divorcees are his most vulnerable female prey, but no one is really safe.

His favorite come-on lines are, "You're the type of gal who'd look *stunning* in a time-share," and, "Because I like you so much, I'm going to make you a *special* offer!"

Warning signs that you're dealing with this creature: He sells condos in the Everglades or homes with basements in Miami Beach. And "extremely pushy" is listed as a strength on his resume.

Florida's Snakey Sam
(swampsalesmanus amongus)

Preppy Palmer *(purebredus the-thirdus)*

Most commonly found in Palm Beach, this species is easy to spot. Just look for someone wearing khakis, a pink Polo shirt, and a blue blazer, who calls himself something like "Biff" or "Chip." (His parents gave him a stuffy name like Harrington, Sanford, or Palmer, but he prefers a name that shows what a really "fun guy" he is.)

Preppy Palmer's daddy taught him that the solution to any problem is to throw money at it — and his mother taught him the importance of insulating himself against all the lower, more common life forms in the universe.

His idea of roughing it is drinking water without lemon.

If you date a Preppy Palmer, he'll wine you and dine you. But don't even think about marriage unless your Mumsie and Daddums have buildings named after them at Harvard or Yale.

Florida's Preppy Palmer
(purebredus the-thirdus)

Fraternal Fred *(alpha-beta-chi-omegus secret-handshakus)*

Found mainly in homogeneous groupings in Tallahassee and Gainesville, Fraternal Freds are the most daring of the male species. They'll do *anything* to impress their "brothers."

Fraternal Freds dwell 4-to-a-cage, and adorn these habitats with elaborate collections of imported beer cans (each one recalling a fond memory) and posters raising Cindy Crawford to goddess level.

The fun part about dating a Fraternal Fred is that you'll instantly inherit 126 of his very loyal brothers. They're so loyal, in fact, that if Fred can't make your date, one of them will.

A Fraternal Fred at a later stage of development (perhaps five years after graduation) is your best bet. He'll be ready to switch his loyalties to you.

Florida's Fraternal Fred
(alpha-beta-chi-omegus secret-handshakus)

Aristocratic Art *(lookus down-his-noseus)*

This intellectual, well-mannered species can be found exploring Florida's museums, libraries, theaters, and sights of historic interest.

He buys his wine in France, his shoes in Italy, and his cars in Sweden. He speaks a multitude of languages fluently, and even his English sounds imported.

If you share Aristocratic Art's disdain for anyone who doesn't pronounce "grimace" (gri-'mays) correctly, this could be the man for you. However, if you stayed away from *Hot Shots, Part Deux* because you thought it was a foreign film — forget it.

Florida's Aristocratic Art
(lookus down-his-noseus)

Wonder Phil *(perfectus manus)*

Wonder Phil is the rarest of all the breeds — the kind of man that every woman dreams of meeting.

He is generous, ambitious, courteous, gracious, and monogamous. When he sees you, he turns the game off and asks how you are. He insists on going to visit *your* family for the holidays (as long as that's what *you* want to do). He is blinded to all women except you. He loves to buy you gifts, cook dinner for you, and clean up the kitchen afterward. And when he says he'll call you, he means as *soon* as he gets home.

If you find this treasure, snag, tag, and mate immediately!

Florida's Wonder Phil
(perfectus manus)

Chapter 2

True Stories, Part I

Tales From the Zoo

A confrontation with a member of the male species brings out the best in every female. We respond either with the "sight/fright" reflex, the urge to kill, or (with any luck) the mating instinct.

This is how some of the women we interviewed described their experiences:

• *A cautionary tale about a first — and last — date with a Gameboy Gary:*

I met "Gary" at a sporting goods store. He had a great body. It was obvious that he was listening to the FSU-Miami game, so, being a Seminole fan myself, I asked him the score. We started to talk, and realized we lived in the same neighborhood. When he asked me out, I looked forward to a romantic evening with this super-hunk.

He walked in looking like a walking sports billboard. He wore Seminole shorts (in my honor, he said), a Tampa Bay Buccaneers hat, and a sweatshirt that read, "Football Is For Studs." Before I could get into the car, I had to clear away a tennis racket, some power food wrappers, three copies of "Sports Illustrated," and a stack of Orlando Magic ticket stubs.

He took me to a sports bar where all his buddies were hanging out with their girlfriends, and he spent the whole night betting on games with his friends while I made small talk with women I didn't know.

At the end of the evening, he told me what a great time he had, and asked if he could walk me to the door. I said, "No thanks, I can do that alone, too." He had no idea what I was talking about.

My score for Gameboy Gary: Zero!

— Sandra, Sarasota

● *Chivalry on wheels — the perfect example of what could happen if you meet up with Harley Hank:*

I was on my way to work when my car stalled — at 7:30 in the morning. I was looking under the hood (though I don't know anything about cars, so I'm not exactly sure what I was looking for) when this tough-looking guy on a motorcycle pulled up next to me and asked if I needed help.

He pushed my car off the road, and since we weren't too far from my mother's house, I asked him for a ride. (I figured if he tried anything, I could jump off the motorcycle.) When we got to my mother's, he asked for my phone number. He called the next day, and we started dating.

Now we're married and have two children — and his-and-hers cycles.

— Yolanda, Miami

• *A date with Earlybird Ernie may be stress-free, but it's not entirely without risk:*

On our first date, "Ernie" took me to Shoney's (for the early bird special). We were having a lovely time when, midway through the soup course, I heard a clank and a splash. His teeth had fallen into the soup!

— Eleanor, Jacksonville

• *Vanity Vince — a model boyfriend:*

"Vince" has the prettiest face of anyone — male or female — that I know. He has a tiny nose, deep blue eyes with long black lashes, and baby-soft skin. I don't think he could grow a beard if he drank testosterone.

When I started dating him, he was working as a carpenter, and I was making a pretty good living as an actress. One day, "Vince" had nothing else to do, so he joined me on a casting call for a soft drink commercial in Fort Lauderdale. I was pretty confident that I had done well, so I wasn't surprised when the director called a few days later.

But it wasn't me he wanted — it was "Vince"! And when "Vince" found out they were offering him twice as much money to use his face as he had been making with his hands, he kissed carpentry (and me) goodbye.

— **Jill, Vero Beach**

• *A failed attempt at a relationship with a Cellular Sal:*

"Sal" seemed to be a nice guy, but I never really got to know him, because he didn't get off the phone long enough.

That phone drove me crazy! No matter where we were — at any time of day or night — it kept going off. He always jumped up to take the call, whether it was a business call, a personal call, or a wrong number. (I could understand the urgency if "Sal" were a doctor — but he's an insurance salesman.)

I reached my breaking point one evening when the phone rang in the middle of a romantic dinner at a very fancy restaurant. It was one of "Sal's" friends asking him if he wanted to go in on some basketball tickets. I glanced at my watch, and started to time the conversation. After 15 minutes, I had had enough.

I got up from the table, and headed toward the door. "Sal" ran after me (with the phone still pressed to his ear), saying "Where are you going?"

"To get an unlisted number," I replied as I made a satisfyingly dramatic exit. And that was the end of that.

— **Cindy, Palm Beach**

- *With Rico Suave, possession is ten-tenths of the law:*

"Rico" is a security guard at the hospital where I work — a tall, dark, handsome Latino with a great smile. He caught my eye the first time I entered the building. Before long, we were exchanging "hellos" and "goodbyes." Then we moved on to comments about the weather, and conversations about work. Finally, he asked me out.

We had some time to kill before the movie that we wanted to see started, so we went to a nearby pool hall where "Rico" is a regular.

He knew almost everyone in the place, and his buddies kept stopping by to chat with us. I didn't want to be unfriendly, so I joined the conversation. Bad idea!

When we left the pool hall, "Rico" said, "Forget the movie. I'm taking you home."

At first I thought he was joking, but when he curled his lip and added, "I saw the way you were looking at my friends," I knew that I had done something terribly wrong — though I wasn't exactly sure what.

So now I sneak in the back entrance when I go to work.

— **Jennifer, Pompano Beach**

- *When Hurricane Andrew blows into town, watch out:*

The first indication I had that there was a problem was when a girl came up to my boyfriend

"Andrew" and said, "Omigod, Larry! What are you doing here? How's your mother?"

Then we went to Paradise Island for the weekend, and another girl came up and said, "Larry! Is your mother OK? How did the surgery go?" Then she pointed at me and asked, "Who is this?"

"Andrew" responded to both of these confrontations by dragging me away, insisting they must be confusing him with someone else.

But then I spotted "Andrew's" face on a "Most Wanted" poster in the post office — and called the police. Turns out "Larry" (one of his aliases) was wanted for murder in another state. And every time he thought the police were on his trail, he'd tell his current girlfriend that his mother back in Ohio was in the hospital and he had to go.

He's now serving time in a state prison.

— **Linda, North Miami**

• *Snakey Sam — Mr. "Right Now":*

"Sam" told me he wasn't looking for an affair — he wanted a relationship, something solid. And he wanted children. Lots of them.

On our first date, he exclaimed that he didn't believe in waiting. He said he had traveled all around the world and dated all sorts of women, and he was certain that I was the right one for him.

When I reminded him that we had only known each other for 45 minutes, and explained that I really needed to get to know him better before making a lifetime commitment, "Sam" turned on some soft *music and asked me to dance. Then he dashed out of the room, and came back with a stack of pamphlets about time-share properties.*

He told me he would love me very much, and that we would be very happy together if I invested in a time-share with him.

When I said that I had absolutely no interest in the property, he wished me the best of luck and disappeared.

— **Marcia, Jupiter**

• *An affair to remember — a date with Fraternal Fred:*

My boyfriend's semi-formal was held at a major hotel in town — very posh! He and a bunch of his "brothers" rented a room there so we could do some private partying.

We were all drinking quite a bit, so I guess that explains why no one noticed when "Fred" slipped out of the room. But we certainly did notice when security knocked on our door, and delivered "Fred" — wrapped in a towel.

Seems "Fred" had been riding up and down the hotel's glass elevator, flashing all the guests. He claims to remember nothing of this incident — but I bet the folks who witnessed it can't say the same.

— **Karen, Fort Myers**

Chapter 3

Where the Boys Are

Now That You Know What You're Looking for,
Where Do You Find Him?

Women have as much trouble finding men as they do the perfect bra. And men have as much trouble finding women as they do the ultimate sound system.

4 Reasons Men and Women
Have Trouble Finding Each Other

Men and women have had trouble connecting with each other for at least 250,000 years — and the situation seems to get worse, instead of better, with every passing year. Here's why:

1. We ask the wrong people.

Men ask men, "Where are the girls?" and women ask women, "Where are the guys?" (If they knew the answer to that question, they wouldn't be single.)

2.   We watch too many movies.

We think we don't have to make any effort to find each other — fate will deliver true love into our waiting arms. Our eyes will meet across a crowded room, and romantic lightning will strike. (Get real!)

3.   We're fooling ourselves.

We're independent, self-assured singles of the nineties, so comfortable with ourselves that we say we don't need anyone to make us feel complete. (Really? And do we give ourselves back massages, too?)

4.   We're workaholics.

We're hard-working, ambitious, directed, and we work at least 80 hours a week. If it's not on the daily planner, it doesn't happen. As a result, we wind up disappointed, depressed, and back on the couch contemplating the benefits of abstinence.

If You Want to Find a Guy, You've Got to Think Like a Guy

To direct you to the very best, most reliable hunting grounds, we went directly to the experts. We asked hundreds of men where they hang out, and where they would send their sisters to meet someone. Then we compiled our list.

Now you've got to do a little creative thinking. Study our list, and then ask yourself where you might go if you were the kind of man that you would like to meet. Be sure to consider the time of day, the day of the week, and the season of the year that you're dealing with. It makes a difference.

43 Places
to Find a Man in Florida

1.   Your Grandparents' Condo

Check out the pool next time you go to Grandma's for dinner. If her place is on the beach, chances are her neighbors will be entertaining a promising supply of grandsons and nephews. If you don't have grandparents nearby, find a friend who does. If you can't get into their pool, tan on the beach behind their building.

If you're smart, you'll schmooze with the neighbors before season starts to find out which ones are expecting male relatives in your age range. You'd be surprised how many Florida women meet men this way.

2.   Publix Supermarket

Publix is a great place to meet singles — if you go to the right store at the right time. Choose a store in an area where there are lots of singles around your age. A store near a college campus or a gym, for example, is a great meeting market. Stay away from retirement communities and family neighborhoods (unless you're looking for a "silver fox" or an affair with a married man).

Don't go shopping in the morning, unless you really need to buy food. The best time to go is right after work (around 6 p.m.), or late in the evening (after 9 p.m.). Many stores stay open until 11 p.m. Sunday and Monday nights are great (except during football season). Don't ever shop on Saturday night — much too depressing. The only people who go out for groceries then are couples — very boring couples who have nothing else to do on the weekend.

Remember, a man doesn't shop more than once a week, so you'll need to catch him during one of those rare moments when he's stocking up.

3.   Your High School Reunion

If you went to high school in Florida and your reunion is coming up, don't get a date. Go alone. Many single men go stag. And some of those single men who weren't too appealing 10, 20, or 30 years ago may have blossomed into great date material.

People and circumstances change over the years. Men who were married or "going steady" when you knew them may have become unhitched. And someone you totally ignored in high school may have developed into a much more interesting prospect.

4.   Alumni Associations

Many singles find each other at alumni meetings years after they graduate. So call your alma mater (even if it's out of state), and find out if they sponsor an alumni group near you.

5.   Singles-Only Vacations

Call your travel agent right now and ask about singles-only trips. Whether you're interested in a one-night cruise, a weekend in Key West, or a week of cycling through the Berkshires, this is the only kind of travel that guarantees the men you meet will be single. Be sure to ask ahead of time how many men are signed up.

6.   Casinos and Tracks

We're not suggesting you hook up with a hardcore gambler, but gambling does attract lots of adventurous men. Dog tracks, race tracks, and jai-alai are all worth a visit. So are Florida's Indian reservations that offer limited gambling, and the many cruise ships that offer evening outings.

Try it! Who knows — you might hit the jackpot!

7.   Home Depot or Builders Square

Handy men galore! Next time you need a light bulb, a toilet paper holder, or some paint, go to a home improvement superstore. If you see a guy who looks interesting, strike up a conversation by asking his opinion on that dimmer switch you're thinking about buying. Maybe he'll offer to come over and install it.

8.   Health Clubs and Gyms

If you're thinking about joining a gym, don't join one that's "ladies only." You're not going to meet a guy there. If you think you'd rather not even try to meet someone at the gym because you think you look terrible when you work out, think again. Coed gyms always have more men than women. And if the ratio is 40 to 1 in your favor, he's not going to care if your hair is plastered to your forehead. (If you're really self-conscious about your appearance, do your serious work out early in the morning when the gym is practically empty, and come back later for a light run-through.)

The absolute best time to meet single men at the gym is right after work. If he's not doing his grocery shopping then, he's there. On weekends, try Saturday morning.

Don't hang out in the aerobics studio — too many women. If you want to meet men, you have to be in the nautilus/weight room. When you see someone you like, compliment him on his strength or form. Then ask him for help with your set. Tip: Don't towel dry when you sweat — men think sweat is sexy.

Another thing to keep in mind is that if you run into a guy you recognize from the gym — maybe at Publix or at a club — be sure to say "hello." He may not recognize you in your street clothes, but he'll be flattered that you remembered him, and impressed with you because you care enough about yourself to work out.

9. Night Classes

If you have time to watch *Melrose Place* or to get a manicure once a week, you have time to take a class at your local community college. Check the newspaper for listings, and then sign up for wine tasting, scuba diving, *tae kwon do*, real estate, personal finance — any subject that interests men.

10. Hotels

Florida is the nation's tourist capital, so naturally it's loaded with hotels. Most of them have restaurants, nightclubs, and bars that are open to both tourists and locals. You have a good chance of meeting a guy here that lives in the neighborhood.

11. Driving School

Did you get a ticket for not wearing your seatbelt? Sliding through a stop sign? Speeding? Pay the ticket and opt for driving school. It will save you from getting points on your license, and maybe even get you a date.

When class starts, the teacher may go around the room and ask each one of you what you did to get there. Target the guy with the zippy Porsche that "just kind of got away from him," or the one who forgot to use his turn signal. Avoid anyone who's there for driving under the influence, or for hit-and-run.

12. Bars and Nightclubs

Most people think bars are terrible places to meet men. Not true. And Florida is loaded with them. As of 1990, Florida had almost 400,000 bars and restaurants.

The best bars are sports bars, and bars with happy hours, live music, or pool tables. Even if he hates the bar scene, if his friends are meeting for a drink after work, or to watch the game, or to listen to a favorite band, the bar doesn't seem like a bar to him. Understand?

The best time to go to a bar is on game day. Get there before he does and get a seat near the screen. He won't talk to you while the game is on, but if you start chatting before it starts, he'll remember you when his team scores or during a break. If you're not really interested in sports, at least find out who's playing before you sit down. If you want to be his true fantasy woman, you have to really love the game. But never pretend to be a fan just to impress him. He'll see right through you.

Another good time to hit the bars is on Ladies' Night. Ladies' Nights always have more men than women because when men are guaranteed to find women, they come in droves.

Obviously you don't want to meet a guy who hangs out in neighborhood bars in the middle of the afternoon, or one who trolls the dance clubs at 11:00 on a Tuesday night hoping to get lucky. So just don't be there.

And remember, any place that has at least one pool table has at least two men. Maybe one will be single.

13. Outdoor Concerts
Outdoor rock and jazz concerts are a casual, fun place to meet. But stay away from performers that specialize in romantic love ballads. Every single man in the house will be there with a date.

14. Sporting Goods Stores
When you go to buy your next pair of sneakers, check out the studs fondling the sports equipment. You'll

also find athletic men at specialty stores that sell fishing, diving, tennis, and golf paraphernalia.

15. Pet Supply Stores

We're not talking about the cutesy "doggie in the window" pet stores in the mall. We're talking about serious pet supply stores that sell salt water aquariums, 50-pound bags of high-protein dog food, and 100-pound test training leashes. You'll also find animal-loving men — and their macho dogs — in obedience training classes.

16. Record Stores and CD Exchanges

Next time you're in one of these places, look around. The majority of the customers are men. Stores that sell car and home stereo systems are other good guy spotting spots.

17. Bookstores

Where there are books, there are intellectual men — buying and selling. You'll find interesting men perusing the periodicals or thumbing through the business and sports sections.

18. Libraries

Not all the men in libraries are homeless. Some of them are very good date material. Research libraries at local colleges and universities are especially good meeting grounds. Researchers and professors go there, as well as students. When one of them catches your eye, ask him a question. You'll have to whisper — very sexy!

19. Fundraisers

Many charitable groups sponsor special events and parties to raise money. These functions are often singles parties in disguise. The tickets may be overpriced, but keep in mind that you're spending money on a good cause — you.

20. Walking/Running Races

If you're in shape, enter a 5K or 10K race. (You'll find them listed in your local community calendar.) If you're not physically up to the challenge, volunteer to work the drink or information booth, or to serve water to the participants. Most of the people you'll meet here will be men.

21. Ball Games

Florida is home to many professional and college teams, and is the spring training site for 18 major league baseball teams — known to fans as the "Grapefruit League." The "Grapefruit League" arrives in Florida around the end of February and plays a series of exhibition games through March and early April.

22. Tournaments

Just about any kind of sports tournament from fishing to volleyball is worth a visit.

23. Sports Courts

Wherever you find a sports court — for volleyball, racquetball, tennis, basketball, etc. — you'll find men.

24. The County Courthouse

Courthouses are full of young attorneys, and the surrounding benches and restaurants are packed with them during lunch hour. Spend some time researching the public records (you might meet someone that way, too), and then break for lunch when and where the single guys do.

25. The Beach

You've got plenty to choose from here. Florida has 9,000 miles of beaches. No place in this state is more than 60 miles from salt water — and there are more fresh water lakes than we can count. Find a beach with a volleyball net, and you're guaranteed to find a lot of men who are in great shape.

26. Any place People Rollerblade/Jog/Bicycle

Join in — and you'll meet men.

27. Auto Supply Stores

Don't ask your brother to pick up a gallon of windshield wiper fluid for you. Go yourself. You'll probably be the only woman in the place.

28. Computer Stores

Most of the salespeople and customers in here are men. So go there to price out that new computer you want, and strike up a conversation with the guy standing next to you who's interested in the same machine.

29. Auto Shows and Boat Shows

Is the auto show in town? What about the boat show? Go!

30. Auctions

Check the classifieds every weekend. Auctions attract aggressive, resourceful men.

31. Trading Card Shows

You can find a sports trading card show in town just about every weekend. And they're always filled with men.

32. Churches or Synagogues
Join the choir or attend a lecture. You don't need to be super-religious to attend services or to attend their singles get-togethers.

33. Laundromats
Apartment or neighborhood laundries — especially in college towns — are a great place to meet men. But check out what he's washing before you say, "hello." If there's a trace of lace, try someone else.

34. The Chamber of Commerce
Start to attend meetings. You just might meet a man who owns his own business. And go to chamber-sponsored business card exchanges to make both professional and personal contacts.

35. City Commission Meetings
When there's a cause worth fighting for, you'll meet the exciting activists in your neighborhood. So keep up with the news — and support the issues you believe in.

36. Democrat/Republican Clubs
There's nothing like a man with an interest in politics. He's passionate, intellectual, interesting — what more could you want? If you don't want to join the club, at least attend their next fundraiser.

37. Garage Sales
Read the ads. Men shop garage sales for furniture, electronics, and tools.

38. Hobby Shops
Places that cater to model train and plane enthusi-

asts cater to a mostly male clientele.

39. Neighborhood Parks
They play softball, baseball, and flag football here on weekends. Join them — or cheer them on.

40. Weddings
Next time a friend (or relative) gets married, volunteer to help pick out the tuxes. You'll find loads of men in the formal wear shop. And when you go to the wedding, don't take a date. Instead, sit at the singles table and introduce yourself to all the eligible bachelors.

41. Restaurants
Go out for breakfast or lunch — alone. You'll be very approachable.

42. The Mall
The best time to find men in the mall is during the holidays. You'll find them only in shops that sell electronics, music, sporting goods, or books. In department stores, you'll find them in the menswear section. If you see a single guy that appeals to you, ask him to help you pick out a shirt for your father's birthday — even if it's 10 months away.

43. Do-It-Yourself Car Washes
Some say you can tell how a man will take care of his wife by seeing how he takes care of his car (another version of the "how he treats his mother" principle). That's why you probably want one with the patience and endurance to lovingly wash and wax by hand.
    You'll find him here.

Chapter 4

True Stories, Part II

It's Not Always How You Meet;
It's Who You Meet

Most men and women meet their mates in the usual ways — on a blind date, at a local hangout, or on the job. But there's an unexpected twist to everybody's true-life story.

These are our favorites:

• **They met on a blind date — but not their blind date:**

My boss set me up with his nephew. I met him at a restaurant and we couldn't have been a more mismatched couple. On the phone, he told me he looked like Dustin Hoffman, and he wasn't lying. He did look like Dustin Hoffman — in "Rainman." Worse than that, we had absolutely nothing in common. We had nothing to talk about, so we just stared at each other and ate in awkward silence.

When we finished eating, he paid the check and disappeared. A man sitting alone at the next table leaned over and asked why my date left. I told him it was a blind date from the lowest depths of hell. We talked for about an hour, and had such a good time together that we decided to meet for lunch at the same place the next day.

It's a year later, and we're still eating there — as man and wife.

— Stephanie, Fort Pierce

• *Sometimes the right guy is the wrong guy:*

My car was in the shop, and I had no way of getting to a party my brother Bill was throwing one weekend. So he said he'd send his friend Richard over to pick me up. Since it was raining, I volunteered to wait outside.

A man matching Richard's description pulled up, and started looking around as if he wasn't sure who he was looking for. I ran up, said "hi," and jumped into the car.

He was adorable! And the two of us hit it off immediately. But about 15 minutes into the ride, I realized that we were going the wrong way, and said, "Hey, this isn't the way to Bill's place."

He said, "Who's Bill?"

And I said, "Aren't you Richard?"

And he said, "No, I'm Todd. Aren't you Cindy?"

We drove back to my place, laughing all the way. Sure enough, the real Richard and the real Cindy (Todd's blind date) were there. We tried to explain that we had made an honest mistake, but neither one of them thought that making them wait half an hour in the rain was very funny.

Richard drove me to the party. And Todd took Cindy out for dinner. But he called me the next day — and we've been dating ever since.

— Jackie, St. Petersburg

• ***She got more than she bargained for on this shopping trip:***

After I got divorced, I decided to never get involved with a man again. It's hard enough at 25, let alone 55.

Anyway, about six months ago I was trying on shoes at J.C. Penney, and the salesman, a tall, gray-haired man in his early 60s kept flirting with me — obviously trying to get me to buy shoes. I ended up with six pairs.

There was another pair that I loved, but he didn't have them in my size. He said he would order them from another store and call me when they came in.

Three days later, he called. I said, "Did my shoes come in?" And he said, "No, but would you like to go out for dinner?" I said, "I haven't been on a date in 10 years." And he laughed and said, "I haven't been on one in eight."

We've been dating ever since.

— Sylvia, Tallahassee

● *The fringe benefits of a change of pace:*

I hadn't skated for years, but I had won a lot of ice skating medals when I was young — before I moved to Florida. So, one day when I was really bored with the treadmill at the gym, I had the bright idea to try out the local indoor rink.

As I spun around, trying to remember my old routines, I noticed an attractive man watching me. I thought I'd give him something worth watching, so I started to show off— spinning really fast, and jumping really high. The next thing I knew, he came up behind me, lifted me up over his head, and twirled me around.

Turns out he used to be a champion skater, too. We clowned around on the ice all afternoon, and went out to dinner that night. Six months later, we went to the 1994 Winter Olympics in Norway for our honeymoon.

— **Carrie, Sunrise**

● *She got more than just a tip from this customer:*

John came into the diner where I work at least twice a week and always ordered the same thing — scrambled eggs and hash browns. And he always poured sugar on his eggs. Really drowned them in the stuff.

One day I told him that too much sugar wasn't good for him. He said that no one except his wife had the right to tell him what to eat, so I asked him what his wife thought of his sugar habit. He laughed and said he wasn't married. I said that if I was his wife, I wouldn't let him eat so much sugar — and he asked me to marry him.

I thought he was joking, but he said he'd had his eye on me for years. I told him that people have to date before they get married — so we dated for three weeks and then got married.

— Doris, Jacksonville

• ***They met literally by accident:***

I got into an accident on the way to take my final exams at FSU. I was trapped in my car, and Larry was the paramedic at the scene.

In the emergency room, he asked me if I wanted to have dinner with him sometime. I was trapped in a backboard, wearing a neck brace, flipped over facing down, so I told him to duck down so I could get a better look at him. He looked good — nice blue eyes, long black eyelashes, dark curly hair — so I said "yes."

We had our first date a week after the wreck — and we were engaged two months later.

— Hope, Tallahassee

• ***First, her aunt died. Then, her car died. Then she met John:***

My car got stuck on the way to the cemetery during my aunt's funeral. The police officer who was escorting us called for backup so he could stay with me. I figured he felt sorry for me because I couldn't stop crying.

The next day I went to the police station to thank him (and also because I thought he was cute, and I really wanted to see him again). Before I could think of a subtle way to find out if he was single, he asked me out.

We dated for six months and then got married.

— Jessica, Jacksonville

========= Chapter 5 =========

Playing the
Numbers Game

Increase Your Odds By Knowing the Odds

You'll have a much easier time meeting a man if you know where to find him. After all, if you want to do your networking and partying in his neighborhood, you have to know where his neighborhood is.

So, to help you find the answers to your man-hunting questions, we analyzed the numbers for you. We used data from the latest U.S. Census report on the marital status of men 18 and older living in approximately 50 Florida cities with populations of at least 19,000 (not including unincorporated areas).

The numbers look pretty good to us. You've got a grand total of 842,728 single Florida men to choose from — and an overwhelming percentage of them have never been married!

Here's the breakdown:

Status	Number of Men in This Group	% of All Single Men in Florida
Never Married	559,410	66.38%
Divorced	178,137	21.14%
Widowed	59,936	7.11%
Separated	45,245	5.37%

Now on to more important stuff ...

The Best — and Worst — Places to Find Single Men in Florida

The Top 10 Cities to Find Single Men

Rank	City	Total % of Single Men
#1	Gainesville	62.24%
#2	Tallahassee	59.85%
#3	Orlando	58.92%
#4	Ft. Lauderdale	58.19%
#5	Oakland Park	57.69%
#6	Miami Beach	55.98%
#7	Ft. Myers	55.33%
#8	Miami	55.15%
#9	Key West	54.53%
#10	West Palm Beach	53.98%

Some of these cities also have a high percentage of single women, but don't let that worry you. The important thing is for you to be where the men are. However, forget about Key West. There may be a lot of single men here, but they're interested in all the other single men.

The 10 Worst Cities to Find Single Men

Rank	City	Total % of Single Men
#1	Port St. Lucie	28.16%
#2	Cape Coral	28.59%
#3	Tamarac	29.64%
#4	Coconut Creek	30.81%
#5	Cooper City	30.90%
#6	Pembroke Pines	33.72%
#7	Sunrise	34.45%
#8	Margate	34.77%
#9	Palm Bay	35.43%
#10	Coral Springs	36.14%

Most of these cities are sleepy little family communities. You don't want to live here, even if Mom and Dad still do.

You Say You Want More Statistics?

Take a look at the regional map on the next page ....

Regional Map of Florida

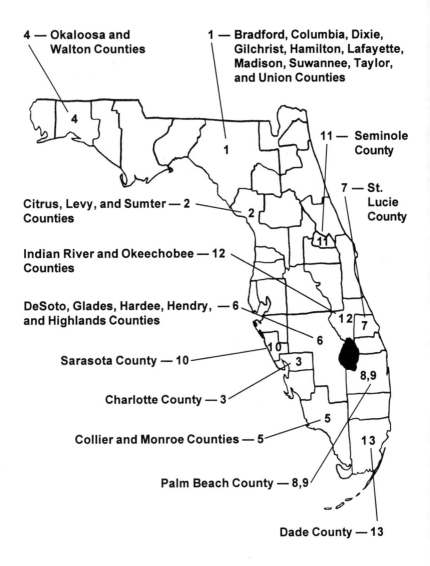

4 — Okaloosa and
    Walton Counties

1 — Bradford, Columbia, Dixie,
    Gilchrist, Hamilton, Lafayette,
    Madison, Suwannee, Taylor,
    and Union Counties

11 — Seminole
     County

7 — St.
    Lucie
    County

Citrus, Levy, and Sumter — 2
Counties

Indian River and Okeechobee — 12
Counties

DeSoto, Glades, Hardee, Hendry, — 6
and Highlands Counties

Sarasota County — 10

Charlotte County — 3

Collier and Monroe Counties — 5

Palm Beach County — 8,9

Dade County — 13

(1) The best ratio of single men to single women of all ages (2 to 1)

(2) The best ratio of single men to single women aged 18 to 24 (2 to 1)

(3) The best ratio of single men to single women aged 25 to 34 (3 to 1)

(4) The best ratio of single men to single women aged 35 to 44 (3 to 1)

(5) The best ratio of single men to single women aged 45 to 54 (7 to 2)

(6) The best ratio of single men to single women aged 55 to 64 (3 to 1)

(7) The best ratio of single men to single women aged 65 and up (2 to 1)

(8) The highest percentage of single men who earn between $30,000 and $49,999 a year (11.3%)

(9) The highest percentage of single men who earn between $50,000 and $79,999 a year (3.2%)

(10) The highest percentage of single men who earn more than $80,000 a year (1.3%)

(11) The highest percentage of single men with a college degree (15.5%)

(12) The highest percentage of single men with a Ph.D. (1.4%)

(13) The highest percentage of single professionals — doctors, lawyers, etc. (2.5%)

═════════ **Chapter 6** ═════════

Meeting Strategies
and Dating Tips

*Once You've Found Him, How Do You Get Him
to Ask You Out — and Keep Asking You Out?*

The real experts on the dating scene in Florida
aren't the pollsters or the personal growth therapists.
The people who really know what they're talking
about are the men and women who have successfully
navigated the dating maze.

So that's who we talked to.

The following meeting strategies and dating tips
were gathered from hundreds of informal interviews.
We asked the men what it was that attracted them to
their girlfriends or wives (and what turned them off
about other women). And we asked the women for
practical advice — tips that they have personally used
to meet eligible men.

25 Meeting Strategies

1. Don't travel in packs.
Even if a guy wants to introduce himself to you, he might be self-conscious or intimidated if you're surrounded by an entourage. You're much more approachable if you're with just one or two friends.

2. Try it solo.
You're at your most approachable when you're alone. True, you probably don't want to go to a bar alone — but try a casual restaurant for breakfast or lunch.

3. Get rid of your negative friends.
Men say even if they like you, if your friends give off negative vibes, it will keep them away. So go out with women who are friendly, attractive, secure, and outgoing. They'll attract men to your table.

4. Introduce yourself.
Don't wait for him. If you like him, walk over and say, "Hi." The worst thing that could happen — he'll blow you off. (You'll live.)

5. Get your friend to introduce you.
Have her walk over and tell him that you'd like to meet him. He'll be flattered.

6. Get his friend to introduce you.
Catch his friend alone, and tell him you'd like him to introduce you. They'll both be flattered.

7. Smile.
Men say if you like them, give them a clue. Look at

him. Smile — at least twice. Give him some sort of a sign that you won't reject him if he approaches you. If he smiles back, you'll know it's safe for you to approach him.

8. Don't take rejection personally.

Meeting the right man is just a matter of meeting enough men. If this one doesn't like you, just keep right on going until you find one who does.

9. Use positive body language.

When you're talking to him, look him in the eye, and relax. Don't play with your napkin, look frantically around the room, or giggle.

10. Don't focus on the most sought-after man in the room.

There's no need to compete with every other woman in the place. Look around. He may not be the first one to catch your eye, but he might be the one to win your heart.

11. Don't reject him for something trivial.

Maybe you don't like his mustache, or the way he holds his fork. A razor and a lesson from Miss Manners can change your dud into a stud overnight. Unless he has a serious flaw that can't be ignored, give him a chance. Love at first sight is nice, but doesn't happen enough.

12. Ask him out first.

Be aggressive. Many women are still uneasy with doing the asking, but most men see this as a sign that you're self-confident. And maybe he just needs that one little push.

13. Don't ask him what kind of car he drives, or what he does for a living.

Let him tell you. Men say if you ask about their cars or jobs during the first five minutes of conversation, they peg you as the superficial, money-grubbing type that they're trying to avoid.

14. Don't be a bitch.

Some women think that men are attracted by women "with an attitude." Not true. They all prefer a friendly woman with a sincere smile.

15. Be yourself.

Don't pretend to be a tennis player if you've never stepped on a court, or a jazz buff if you can't tell the difference between Thelonius Monk and a Benedictine Monk. Be honest about your interests, and be open to his. Nobody likes a phony.

16. Don't get drunk.

There's nothing appealing about a woman who's had a few too many.

17. Get a dog, and walk it often.

Dogs are a great attention-getter — especially manly dogs like shepherds and dobermans.

18. Be unique.

Give him an excuse to come up to you and start a conversation. Wear an unusual piece of jewelry, a hat, or a team shirt.

19. Always have a good time.

Whether you meet someone or not, have fun. If you

look like you're having a good time, he'll probably think you're someone worth meeting.

20. Don't go after a taken man.

Don't go after someone's boyfriend or husband. It's also not a good idea to date someone who used to date one of your friends — unless you check with your friend first and she says it's okay. You don't ever want to lose a friend or hurt another woman over a man.

21. Don't try to meet someone if you're in a bad mood.

You won't have a good time, and neither will anyone around you.

22. Don't try to meet someone if you're not ready.

If you just broke up a relationship, you need some time to heal. Men don't want to meet someone who's still hung up on someone else.

23. Change your routine.

If you've been hanging out at the same happy hour every Friday night for the past two months and you haven't met anyone worthwhile, it's time to change your routine. Try new places — a new nightspot, dry cleaner, deli, grocery store, or jogging route. Or try the same old places at different times.

24. If you're really serious about meeting someone, treat it like a job search.

Get out of the house as often as possible. Go to every party you're invited to, and let everyone you know (from your dry cleaner to your great aunt Sadie) that you're available and looking. And make sure your family and friends are carrying around your most recent photo — not the one taken when you still had braces.

25. Never give up.

Don't say you'll never go out on another blind date, or go to another humiliating singles dance, or try another dating service. Go to every party that you hear about, and grab onto every opportunity that comes your way. You *will* meet somebody.

25 Dating Tips

1. Don't complain.

Men complain about women complaining more than anything else.

2. Have something to say.

Men say that too many women expect them to carry the conversation. If you like him, make sure you come up with things to talk about before he runs out.

3. Don't make him plan every date by himself.

Take the initiative, and contribute some of your own ideas from time to time.

4. Make it clear whether you do or don't want to be kissed goodnight.

This is the most awkward moment of every first date, and men say it's easier for women to direct the move. They're always afraid they'll come on too strong, or not strong enough. A peck on the cheek is often appropriate for a first date. But if you feel uncomfortable, stick out your hand for a handshake. He'll get the message.

5. If you want to see him again, be specific.

Don't say something like, "Let's get together again soon" — he'll think "soon" means "never."

6. Suppress your bad habits.

Very few men find anything appealing about women who smoke, swear, gossip, bite their nails, act dumb, twirl their hair, chew gum, or pick their teeth.

7. Unlock his car door.

If he opens your car door for you, unlock his door once you're inside the car. Guys take this as a sign that you're thoughtful and considerate.

8. Compliment him.

Don't just expect him to give you compliments all the time. If he looks great or comes up with a great idea, tell him.

9. Don't order a salad as a main course.

If he takes you out for lunch or dinner, order something besides salad. Men love women who eat — they see it as a sign of passion.

10. Don't order the most expensive item on the menu.

He may take you to the most expensive restaurant in town on your first date, but that doesn't mean that you have to order the filet mignon. If you're unsure of his budget, ask him to recommend something.

11. Say, "Thank You."

Men say that women expect them to pay for everything, but then don't even bother to say "thanks." Sure, he asked you out — but that doesn't mean you can't show your appreciation.

12. Don't have sex with him too soon.

If you sleep with him too soon, he'll question your character, and maybe wonder how special you think he is. So hold off.

13. Don't show him off.

Until you're sure the two of you are an item, don't start bringing him to family functions or dragging him to your friends' weddings.

14. Don't assume he's your repairman.

The best way to get him to help is to let it be his idea.

15. Don't play head games.

If you like him, act like you do. If you don't like him, don't go out with him. If, after a few dates, you don't really want to go out with him anymore, tell him. That way, you won't lead him on, and no one gets hurt.

16. Don't act desperate.

Don't talk about how much you want to get married and have children on the first date. Don't invite him over for a home-cooked meal on the second date. Don't hang all over him when you see him, or call him at work every hour on the hour. Be cool. Give him space and time.

17. Don't overdo the make-up and perfume.

Men prefer the natural look.

18. Don't dress provocatively on the first date.

Don't give him the wrong idea. Save the black mini

skirt and see-through lace blouse for another time.

19. Take the time to look as good as you can.

If you just got home from the gym, take a shower and change before your date. If you don't have time to go home and change after work, bring a change of clothes and toiletries with you to the office.

20. Be ready on time.

Keeping a guy waiting for more than five minutes is rude and a major turn-off. When he gets to your place, you should be dressed and ready to go.

21. Don't talk about your old boyfriends, money, dieting, suntans, your fingernails, or your hair.

Men hate it.

22. Don't talk about yourself all night.

Ask him about him.

23. Don't compare him to anyone else.

He's not anyone's clone, nor do you want him to be.

24. Be honest.

Let him know early on if you've been married or if you have children. If he likes you, those things won't matter.

25. Don't waste your time.

If you've been dating him for two, five, or 10 years, and he still tells you he's not ready to commit, move on. Life is too short to be wasting your time with the wrong man.

Chapter 7

True Stories, Part III

First, You've Got to Get His Attention

The best way to approach a man who interests you is to come up with a reason to start a conversation. Any excuse will do.

Here's what we mean:

- ***Other women may have met men who were drawn to them because of their hair — but not like this:***

I was at this bar in Palm Beach, and at the time, the Tina big-hair look was really in. My hair was everywhere — in this big stiff "do" — and I had to keep flipping it back to keep it out of my face. Then this guy behind me started to tug on it. I tried to

93

ignore him, but he wouldn't stop, and it was really starting to bother me.

I turned around to say something — and realized that my hair was stuck in his straw. The poor guy was just trying to get my hair out of his drink, and I was ready to smack him!

Needless to say, that gave us something to talk about. We started to date, and eventually got married.

— Jodi, North Miami

• **She probably wouldn't have grabbed his attention if it hadn't been for that phone call:**

When this guy sat down next to me at the bar, he said, "Hi, my name's Gerry — what's yours?"

"Candace," I replied, and we started a casual conversation that was really going nowhere until the phone rang at the other end of the bar.

When the bartender held up the phone and asked if there was a Mr. Ford at the bar, Gerry waved him down and took the call. When he hung up, I said, "I don't believe it. Your name is Gerry Ford — as in President Gerald Ford?" And he was instantly annoyed.

"People have been making fun of my name every since Ford took office in the '70s," he said, and got up to leave.

"I understand exactly what you mean," I said.

"How could you possibly understand with a name like 'Candace'?" he grumbled.

"Candace Cane," I replied. "As in Candy Cane."

That did it. He asked for my number, and we've

been dating for the past 10 months.

— Candace, Fort Lauderdale

• **If you like something about a man, just walk right up to him and tell him:**

I love bald men. I have a thing for them. I was at this Top-40 dance club in Miami Lakes, and I saw this bald man dancing with this other woman. I don't know what got into me (maybe a couple of drinks), but I ran over to him while he was dancing with her, grabbed him, kissed his bald head, and screamed, "I just love bald men!"

Three days later, I was at the same club, and he was there alone. He, of course, remembered me, and asked me to dance.

We've been married for 12 years.

— Maggie, Miami

• **Where there's smoke, there's sometimes more than fire:**

I raced out of the shower, and out of my apartment when I smelled smoke and discovered flames shooting up my kitchen wall. I had stupidly forgotten to turn off the burner under a greasy pan. I also forgot that I was wearing nothing but a towel. I ran out into the hall, banging on all the doors until someone — Rob — finally answered.

"You've got to come to my apartment," I cried, "It's on fire!"

He calmly replied, "I'm impressed. That's a much

more creative pick-up line than 'What's your sign?'"

But then he smelled the smoke, and sprang into action. He grabbed the nearest fire extinguisher, charged down the hall, and had the fire out in no time.

The next day, Rob showed up at my door in a towel, and said, "Listen, I've got this really great fire in my apartment that I want to show you."

That night, we went out on our first date.

— Liz, Stuart

* ***They had a "formal" introduction:***

I went to an American Cancer Society theme party called the Tennis Shoe Ball, where everyone dresses up in a combination of clothes they would wear to a formal event, and clothes they would wear on the tennis court. I wore a formal gown and purple high-top sneakers.

After the party, some of us stopped off at a bar — where I met Craig. He started a conversation with me by asking me why on earth I was wearing this outfit, and things took off from there.

We got married about a year later. (Craig wore purple high-tops with his tux.)

— Cherie, Lakeland

Chapter 8

Alternative Ways to Meet Men

When the Time Has Come
to Seek Outside Help

You say you've done everything humanly possible to meet a man? You've been to every bar on ladies night, you've taken adult education classes in accounting and computer programming, and you've even considered joining the Army?

Well, don't give up yet. You haven't even begun to take advantage of some of the best possible ways to meet a man in Florida until you've tried the following creative methods.

1. Personals

Once regarded as a last-ditch effort for geeks and misfits, using the personals has emerged as an acceptable — even trendy — way to meet a man in the '90s.

A majority of the singles that we interviewed for this book (especially South Floridians) said that they feel comfortable with this approach (though they may not admit it).

For example, Laurie, from Boca Raton, told us:

> *My friends call me "Queen of the Personal Ads" because I've gone on more than 300 dates over the past few years with men I've met through the personals. I've gone to rock concerts, out for lobster dinners, and on yacht trips on first dates with these men. My relationships have lasted from four minutes to three months.*

The story that Betsy, from Orlando, told us should give you even more encouragement and inspiration if you're still reluctant to try the personals — even though it was her parents who answered the ad:

> *My parents were always bugging me to answer one of those personal ads, but I didn't want to. I thought it was just for real desperate types — and I hadn't reached that stage yet. Then one day my parents told me they wanted to fix me up with one of their friend's sons. Little did I know that they had found Brad in the personals.*
>
> *He turned out to be exactly my type — about 5'8" with brown curly hair and big blue eyes. He was made to order. After we had been dating for a while, I asked my parents how they knew his parents since they had never mentioned them before. That's when they confessed that they found Brad in the personals, but I was hooked by then, so it didn't bother me.*

We got married a year later, and to this day, most people don't know how we met.

The Most Effective Way to Use the Personals

Men tend to be much more willing to respond to personal ads than women, so we recommend that you place an ad. You're almost guaranteed to get a good response — and you'll save money. Newspapers and singles magazines make money when people respond to their personals (through a 900 number that typically costs $1.99 or more a minute), so they often give away space for free or at a nominal cost to get in as many ads as possible.

Here's How It Works

Don't worry if you're not a gifted writer. The people who take your ads will almost always help you write them at no extra cost. Remember, it's to their financial advantage to help you write ads that will stand out and attract callers.

When you place your written ad, you'll also record a brief message on a private voice mailbox line. When a man responds to your ad, he'll listen to your recorded message, and then leave his own message for you. You'll be able to access your messages by using a private security code.

You can call back the ones that sound good — and dodge the ones that don't. Keep in mind that you're probably going to get a lot of responses — so be selective. Even so, you may have to go on at least a dozen dates before you meet someone who clicks with you.

Secrets of Personal Ad Writing

Whether you write your ad yourself, or get help, make sure your ad includes the following:

• A jazzy headline. One that says, "Here I am! Stop! Read me!"

• One or two attention-getting comments, like "Hurry, this ad will self-destruct soon!" or "Finally! Someone to take home to Mom and Dad."

• An accurate, specific description of what you're looking for. Don't waste valuable ad space trying to sound like something you're not — and don't try to attract every possible size, shape, and style of man. Be honest about your interests. For example, if you're 5'9", maybe you want to limit your search to men who are at least six feet tall. And if you'll date only men who are Christian, non-smokers, or college-educated, make sure you say so.

Advice From the Pros

Newspapers and singles magazines generally don't screen people who place or respond to their ads, but many offer this advice:

• Don't spend too much time on your first phone conversation with him. It will only build up your expectations. Just ask some basic questions and plan your first meeting.

Ask things like "Are you employed?" and "Why did you respond to my ad?" and "What kind of a girl are you looking for?" And double-check to make sure he meets your requirements. For example, if your ad says that you're looking for a 20- to 25-year-old body builder, you don't want to waste your time with a 45-year-old, overweight businessman who is hoping to change your mind.

• Your first meeting should last no more than an hour. Get together for a quick bite or a drink. Use this time to try to figure out if the two of you are compatible. Discuss your likes and dislikes, and your goals. Pay attention to the way he treats the waiter or waitress, the way he carries himself, and the way he carries on a conversation.

If you get the wrong vibes from him, trust your gut instinct and go no further.

• If you would like to see him again, tell him you'll call him. Don't be too quick to give out your home phone number, or too much information about your personal life.

• Don't let him pick you up at home, or make you travel to a place you're not familiar with. Meet at a mutually acceptable public place until you feel that you know him well enough to feel comfortable with him.

Some Personals to Try

• *The Bachelor Book*
Includes about 100 profiles of men around the country, from stockbrokers to postal workers. A 5-issue subscription costs $26.25. Call 800-766-7557 or 305-341-8801 to order.

If you're interested in being included in *The Bachelorette Book*, a companion publication, send a self-addressed stamped envelope to *The Bachelorette Book*, 8222 Wiles Rd., Coral Springs, FL 33607. Costs $75 for subscribers to *The Bachelor Book*, $100 for non-subscribers.

- *Creative Loafing*
  An alternative Tampa Bay publication. Pick up a copy, or call 813-286-1600.

- *Florida Sports Magazine*
  Includes personals from athletes and people who want to meet other active people. You can pick up a free copy at most Florida gyms.

- *Jewish Journal*
  A Miami publication that includes personals. Pick up a copy, or call 800-783-1131 for information.

- *New Times Romance*
  The best personals in Miami. Call 305-579-1550 for information.

- *Singles Choice*
  A magazine for South Florida singles that includes personals. Call 305-424-7855 for a subscription or for ad information. Or write to *Singles Choice*, P.O. Box 16627, Plantation, FL 33318-6627.

- *Singles Serendipity*
  A Jacksonville magazine that includes personals. Pick up a copy at local bookstores and magazines.

- *TeleCompanions*
  A free, 24-hour-a-day talk line. Call 305-933-6868 in Dade, or 305-433-7587 in Broward on your touch-tone phone. Depending on what kind of relationship you're looking for, you'll be instructed to press a key: "1" for long-term, "2" for casual, "3" for exotic adventures, "4" for just phone talk, or "0" for live conversation.

- *XS*

  An alternative Fort Lauderdale paper that draws personal ads from all over South Florida. Call the Love Lines, 800-952-5499.

2. Dating Services

Dating services are becoming popular with professionals all over the country who simply don't have the time to meet someone — and they're especially popular in Florida because so many men and women here are new to the state and don't have many local contacts.

Florida has hundreds of services. Some target only singles within a certain age group, demographic area, or religious affiliation. Others specialize in matching foreign men with American women. Though most simply rely on information they gather during personal interviews or via extensive questionnaires, others use everything from photos, to videos, to computers to match up couples.

Now, maybe you don't like the idea of paying somebody to get you a date, but keep in mind that the matchmaking profession has been around for thousands of years — because it works. It worked for Jamie:

> *I went to every single party in Palm Beach. I networked through friends. I went to charitable functions. I was doing everything right, but I never met anyone worthwhile.*
>
> *Then I got this flyer in the mail from a video dating service. It was expensive — $2,000 for a one-year membership — but they seemed to have a high success rate. I also liked the fact that they screen all the guys, make sure they're not married, and check their backgrounds. So I decided to try it.*

I joined in June. I wrote a profile, describing what I was looking for, brought in a photo of myself, and taped a video. Then I looked through their library of photos to pick out men that appealed to me, and viewed their videos. (If there's a photo with no video, you can guess there's probably something wrong with the guy.) Whenever I found one I liked, they called him up to come in and watch my video. If he liked me, they set us up.

I went on eight dates over the next five months. I chose more than eight guys, but some that I picked weren't interested in meeting me. One man that I met (though it didn't work out), was a doctor who told me the reason he decided to try a dating service was that he didn't get much time out of the office, and wanted to meet someone.

Finally, in November, I met Brian. We dated for about nine months, and then one night he picked me up in a limousine. In the limo, he poured me a glass of champagne, and then got down on his knees and asked me to marry him. We had a white rose wedding, and went to Hawaii for our honeymoon — 13 months from the day we met.

How to Pick a Dating Service

The major hitch in using a dating service is the cost. Florida services charge anywhere from $500 to $3,000, depending on the length of your membership, the prior success of the service, and the size of their database (which can range from 100 to 5,000 members). And at least one South Florida service charges extra if a couple they introduce gets married — $2,500 apiece! So shop around to make sure you're getting a fair deal.

• Contact at least three services in your area. Make sure you understand (and are comfortable with) the methods they use before you consider joining.

• You want to sign with the service that is most likely to be able to help you, so ask each one that you're considering if there's a certain type of woman, or a certain age group that they're most successful with.

• Keep in mind that many dating services don't rely on photos or videos. They make personal judgments based on information they gather during personal interviews. So before you sign with a service that uses this method, make sure they know what they're doing.

• Ask how long they've been in business — and how many marriages they're responsible for. Ask if you can talk to one of their members, and ask if they will refund your money if they get you zero dates. (You should expect from one to 10 dates a month from most dating services.)

• If a service uses photos, ask to see some that are representative of all their members — not just the show album with the best ones.

• Pay in installments if you can — and read every word of your contract.

One Final Word

Ask all your questions, and make sure you get thorough, satisfactory answers before you sign on the dotted line. If you feel at all pressured, give it a little more thought. A successful, reputable company has no need to push you into a contract.

3. Singles/Networking Groups

There are thousands of groups in this state that exist solely for the purpose of getting people together. Some are blatantly geared towards matchmaking. Others are a bit more subtle — like networking groups that sponsor get-togethers to help business people make connections, or volunteer groups that host happy hours and theme parties to support local museums and other non-profit organizations. No matter what their stated purpose, all of them manage to get a lot of single people with similar interests together.

There's Something — and Someone — for Everyone

In the Appendix at the end of this book, you'll find pages and pages of Florida singles and networking groups. You'll find organizations that cater to young professionals, senior citizens, sports enthusiasts, art and music lovers, vegetarians — just about everyone.

Hook up with the right bunch — one that's likely to attract the kind of man that you're looking for — and you'll meet your match.

4. Online Networking

Welcome to the newest way to meet men — via personal computer. All the leading online services have channels that act as mini-clubs. Just find a topic that interests you, and join in. (If you're new to this kind of thing, make sure you read your "help" file first to learn the rules of "netiquette" before you sign on.)

If you make contact with someone who you think you'd like to meet in person, use a little caution — just as you would if you met him through the personals. Remember, you really don't know anything about him except that he knows how to use a computer.

The Leading Online Services

Contact the following services for more information about online networking:

- **America Online**
  8619 Westwood Center Dr.
  Vienna, VA 22182
  Phone: 800-827-6364

- **CompuServe**
  5000 Arlington Centre Blvd.
  P.O. Box 20212
  Columbus, OH 43220
  Phone: 800-848-8199

- **Delphi Internet Services**
  1030 Massachusetts Ave.
  Cambridge, MA 02138
  Phone: 800-695-4005

- **Genie**
  401 N. Washington St.
  Rockville, MD 20850
  Phone: 800-638-9636

- **Prodigy**
  445 Hamilton Ave.
  White Plains, NY 10601
  Phone: 800-284-5933

Chapter 9

True Stories, Part IV

Close Encounters of the Worst Kind

We've all been victims of dating disasters — terrifying ordeals that almost made us give up on the opposite sex. Here are some of the horror stories we heard from women we talked to:

- ***The cheapest man alive:***

  When I met Jason in the parking lot of a local bar, I knew he looked familiar, but I just couldn't place him. Then, when I saw his black convertible Corvette, I remembered — he had dated my sister a couple of years ago. She used to complain about how cheap he was. She said she thought the only reason he had such a nice car was because he skimped on everything else. That's why I was surprised when he took

109

me to the most expensive Italian restaurant in town.

He was very sweet. He requested a special corner table with a view of the restaurant's gardens. He recommended some special dishes from the menu, and ordered a $50 bottle of wine. We talked non-stop, and had a really great time.

At the end of the meal, the bill arrived. I waited and waited for him to pick up the check, but he totally ignored it. We were running out of conversation, and I didn't know what to do, so I excused myself and went to the bathroom. I figured he'd take care of it while I was gone. But it was still there — at my end of the table — when I got back.

Finally, he said, "How about you get this one and I'll get the next one?"

I couldn't believe it! What nerve! But, wimp that I am, I didn't say a word. I just put it on my credit card and wound up paying it off over three months. And when he called and asked me out for a second date, I said, "Sorry, I can't afford it," and hung up.

— Stacey, Orlando

• *We're surprised they didn't meet in Victoria's Secret:*

I dated Sam for about three months when I came across a pair of pink ruffled panties and a matching bra hanging in his shower. When I accused him of seeing someone else, he said the undies belonged to him. He said that sometimes, to relieve stress, he'd slip them on. He said he never wore them outside the house, but he liked the way they felt on his body after a long, hard day.

I didn't believe him, but a close friend of his veri-
fied the story. He told me that Sam isn't gay — he
just likes lacy lingerie. I tried to be understanding,
but I really couldn't deal with dating a guy whose
underwear is prettier than mine.

— Heidi, Tallahassee

• *Talk about credit card abuse:*

My live-in boyfriend was drinking and got in a
car accident on his way home. The only reason he
didn't end up in jail is because I have connections at
the police department.

The officer who picked him up called me and said,
"We've got your boyfriend here. If you want to save
the $250 bail, come and get him."

When I got to the scene, Al was passed out, and
the car was a mangled mess. I looked inside to see if
there was anything in there that might be stolen if we
left it there, and noticed some credit card receipts on
the floor. Considering the fact that his finances were
in such disarray, I thought it was kind of odd that
he'd have credit cards. So I took a closer look.

He had been using my credit cards. The ones I
had been keeping tucked away in a drawer so I
wouldn't use them. He had used my Shell card to fill
up on gas, my Visa to buy drinks for everybody at a
local bar, and my Bloomingdale's card to buy my
birthday present!

I was too embarrassed to press charges — I just
threw him out.

— Kathy, Fort Lauderdale

- *Watch out if he tells you he's a real animal lover:*

I went out with a horse trainer who only kissed me on my forehead. It was the strangest thing. At the end of every date, he would hold my face, and just when I thought he was going to plant one right on my mouth, he'd pull my head down and kiss my forehead.

At first, I thought it was kind of sweet. Sort of the way my grandfather used to kiss me after reading me a bedtime story. But then one day, I showed up at his place while he was grooming one of his horses. He finished, and then gave her a big, wet kiss on the lips.

It was disgusting!

— **Francie, Ocala**

- *Compassion has its limits:*

On my first date with Tim, we decided to meet for drinks. Tim was kind of nervous and had a few too many. He said he wasn't feeling well, and asked if he could put his head on my shoulder. The next thing I knew, he was throwing up in my pocket.

He called the next day to apologize — but I had had enough.

— **Patty, Fort Lauderdale**

- *His mother probably cuts his meat for him, too:*

My brother fixed me up with his tennis partner, Jerry. We had a wonderful conversation on the phone, and made plans to see a movie the following Saturday.

When I answered the door, I discovered that Jerry hadn't come alone. He was there with his mother. While she used my bathroom, he said, "I hope you don't mind. She didn't have anything to do tonight, so I invited her to join us."

We went to the movies (to see "Mrs. Doubtfire"), and had a very good time in spite of the fact that his mother was trailing along behind us.

But he never called me.

I found out from my brother that Jerry said his mother didn't like the way I kept my bathroom.

— Brenda, Gainesville

- *A man with a one-track mind:*

I've met men obsessed with cleanliness, cars, sports, work, and their mothers. But the doozie of them all was the one who was obsessed with Barry Manilow.

He did look a little like Barry — and it was obvious right from the start that he knew it. On our first date, he played Barry Manilow music all night, and made several references to how he would like to spend a "weekend in New England." We got lost on the way to dinner, and when we finally found the restaurant, he started humming, "looks like we made it."

I probably could have overlooked most of this, but when he mentioned that his dog's name is Mandy, it was a little too much for me.

— Vicky, Palm Beach

- *Different is one thing, but weird is something else entirely:*

I met Mitch through the personals — and he was really strange. For example, he said he had very delicate skin, so he used only pig shearing scissors instead of a razor on his face, and he washed his whole body with a special peppermint soap.

He didn't have a refrigerator in his apartment, just a huge freezer stocked with a supply of soy milk. He carried his own bottled water with him wherever he went, and I never saw him eat anything except tofu with honey.

At first, Mitch's bizarre behavior made him sort of interesting. But after a few dates, I got tired of getting a guilt trip about killing animals every time I ordered something like a tuna sandwich, or even an omelet.

— **Carol, South Beach**

- *He really did have a "little black book":*

Ever have one of those dates when, after a few glasses of wine, your hormones take over from your brain? Well, that's what happened to me on a dinner date with a very handsome congressman from Central Florida who, for his wife's sake, shall remain nameless.

After a very romantic, candlelit dinner, we went back to his hotel room "for a nightcap." When he dimmed the lights, I really began to lose it. And after about five minutes on the couch, things got to the point where he had to run downstairs to buy a condom.

While he was gone, I straightened the pillows on the couch — and came upon a little notebook that he had hidden there. On it was a list of women's names, along with notes on how many times he went out with them before they slept with him, and how good they were in bed. On the last line was my name — with a blank space next to it.

I never sobered up so fast in my life. I scribbled the word "sucker" in the space next to my name, and went home.

— Cathy, Tallahassee

• *Every woman's worst nightmare:*

My mother set me up with her friend's son Marv, and it was the worst date of my life. He took me to a really tacky bar where it looked like I was the only woman in the place who wasn't making money that night. He looked like something that had emerged from the black lagoon, and he had absolutely nothing to say.

I was sure that he must have had an equally miserable time with me. That's why I was stunned when he stopped the car in my driveway, turned to me, and said, "I know sex is an unreasonable request — but is a blow job out of the question?"

— Jenny, Miami

Chapter 10

What Every Single Woman Should Know

Practical Advice From the Field

Tune into any conversation at any Florida bar, beach, dressing room, or gym, and you're going to hear women sharing information with other women. Women love to let other women in on the best of the best — the best bargains, the best hairdressers, and the best stories about people they know. (Unfortunately, men often confuse this very important type of networking with gossip.) Women especially like to help each other out by sharing advice about men — good, solid advice based on personal experience.

The hundreds of women that we interviewed for this book shared their words of wisdom with us, and we now pass that collective wisdom on to you.

1.   The very best way to meet a man — through a mutual friend.

There is no better way to find a man than to be fixed up by someone who knows you both. It's easy, fast, safe, and free.

2. The 10 best ways to start a conversation:

• Say "hi" (with a smile). Men say it only takes that one word.

• If you like a guy sitting at a crowded bar, squeeze in next to him and ask him to order a drink for you.

• If he's playing pool, put some quarters on the table and challenge him to the next game.

• If he's watching the news on the TV at the bar, ask him what he thinks of the big story of the day.

• If you're at a party, ask him how he knows the host or hostess. (And keep in mind that the buffet table is a great place to meet men. The ratio of men to women is always 2 to 1.)

• Find an identifier that you can comment on. For example, if he's on crutches, say, "What happened to you?" If he's wearing a team baseball cap, say, "You must be a _____ fan." If he's wearing a college sweatshirt, say, "Do/did you go to _____ ?" If he answers by saying, "Why, do/did you go there too?", be honest. If you can't say "yes," say, "No, but I wanted to meet you and I thought that would be a good approach."

• Say something funny. Share a good joke, or make a witty observation about something (but not someone) around you.

• Ask for his opinion. Say, "So what do you think of this place?" or "What do you think of the music?"

• Ask for help. Men love to feel needed. Ask him to help you open your drink, use a piece of equipment at the gym, or check your tire pressure at the gas station. (But don't ask him for help with directions because then he'll expect you to leave.)

• Ask where he got something. Say, "Where did you get that drink?" or "Where did you get that shirt?" But, please, please, never say, "Where did you get that smile?"

3. The subtlest approach — exchange business cards.

Exchanging business cards lets him know that you're interested (without making you look too forward). If he doesn't call you right away, call him and invite him to lunch. If sparks don't fly, at least you'll have made a business contact.

4. The best excuse to use if you don't want to date him — the truth.

Don't tell him you have a boyfriend, or that you're not over your last one. And don't give him your number just because you feel sorry for him. If you don't like him, simply say, "Sorry, I'm not interested." Don't insult him by making up stories.

5. 7 signs that he has a girlfriend/wife:

• He doesn't give you his home phone number, just a pager or work number — or he tells you it's easier for him to call you.

• The word "we" is used on his message greeting. Women living alone use "we" for security reasons, but most men don't.

• He makes plans with you very far in advance. He may just be very considerate — or he may need the time to work up an excuse for being out that night.

- He never sees you on holidays.
- He always pays cash, or disposes of receipts immediately to eliminate a paper trail.
- He drives more than one car. One of them may be hers.
- He goes on a lot of business trips. If he uses the old "I'm going out of town on business" line on you, he probably uses it on her, too — when he wants to be with you.

6. The best way to get to a party (or a blind date) — in your own car.

It's always wise to drive yourself. That way, you can leave if you're having a terrible time. If you're going someplace with a group of friends, follow each other in separate cars.

7. 3 things to take on every date:

- Money — in case he didn't bring enough, or left his wallet in his other suit. (And quarters in case you need to use a pay phone.)
- A map — especially if you're going someplace neither one of you has been to before.
- An entertainment guide — in case you can't get into the movie/restaurant you planned on, and he's out of ideas.

8. When to dump him — as soon as it's obvious that he's not worthy of your attention and affection.

The less time you spend with the wrong guy, the better. If he borrows money and doesn't pay you back, or if he borrows too often, cancels dates, hurts you (physically or emotionally), insults you, or in any way makes you feel uneasy — it's time for him to go.

One good test is to see how he treats you when you're sick. If he comes over with aspirin, juice, and magazines, he's a keeper. But if he tells you to call him when you're feeling better, he's not worth your time.

9. 6 Ways to get over him:

• Get rid of all his pictures, clothes, and the gifts that he gave you. Put it all in a box and throw it out, or store it somewhere outside your home. (Not the garage — that's not far enough away.)

• Don't call him. Cold turkey is best. It will hurt more in the beginning, but for a shorter period of time.

• Don't talk about him. If your family or friends bring up his name, tell them you can't talk about him or you'll never get over him.

• Write him a letter, and throw it out. Many women feel they have to tell their exes how they feel over the break-up. That's fine. Let it all out on paper, and throw it away. If you have an uncontrollable urge to mail it, mail it to yourself — and then throw it away.

• Write yourself a letter. Or write about your relationship in the guise of a short story. Describe all the problems that you had and list everything about him that bothered you. Read it whenever you think you want to call him. Chances are you broke up for some very good reasons, and your words will remind you why you're no longer together.

• Emerge yourself in something else. Keeping busy will help you get over him a lot sooner. This is a great time to take up a new hobby, put in some extra time at work, sign up for a night class, spend more time with friends, or start a project (such as redecorating). The more active you are, the easier it will be to move on and eventually meet someone else.

**10. The best way to protect your independence —
protect your assets.**

Never give a man — or anyone else — access to
your bank account, credit cards, or investments. Don't
get a joint bank account with your live-in boyfriend. And
when you get married, make sure that you keep your
own savings and your own credit cards.

11. 4 ways to check on his story:
* If he insists he doesn't have a drinking problem,
but he guzzles at least half a dozen brews every time you
go out, you can check to see if he's ever been arrested
for drunk driving.

Stop by your local driver's license bureau. You'll be
able to verify his birthday and his address, and see if his
physical description matches the one on his record. You'll
also find out about any citations he's received in the state
of Florida.
* To check his driving record by mail, send $3
along with (a) his first and last name, (b), his birth date
and — if possible — his birth year, and (c) his social
security number — if you know it — to the Division of
Drivers Licenses, Neil Kirkman Building #B239, Tallahassee, FL 32399-0575.
* If you suspect he may have some ugly secrets in
his past — or present (like a wife and kids), check him
out at the county courthouse (*his* county courthouse).
You'll find out if he has a criminal history, or if he's ever
been involved in a lawsuit. If he's divorced, you'll be
able to get a copy of his divorce papers. Many Florida
courthouses have user-friendly computer terminals, or
even real, live people that can help you with your search.

If he's not from Florida, call or write to the courthouse in his home county. Get the phone number by

calling information in that state. Dial (area code) 555-
1212.

• To do a criminal background check on him by
mail, send $15 along with (a) his first and last name, (b)
his birth date and — if possible — birth year, and (c) his
social security number — if you know it — to the Florida
Department of Law Enforcement, Att: Criminal Records,
P.O. Box 1489, Tallahassee, FL 32302.

If he's ever been arrested in the state of Florida,
you'll get the date, the reason, and the police report case
number, along with the current status of his case. Armed
with this information, you can write or stop by the police
station that handled his case to get a copy of the report.
That report will give you even more details.

If you have any questions about this service, call 904-
488-5081.

Chapter 11

The Best Places to Find Florida Men

Your City-By-City Guide

1. Boca Raton/Delray/Boynton Beach

Architect Addison Mizner designed Boca Raton in the 1920s for an affluent crowd. But he had no way of knowing that it would ultimately be invaded by an army of yuppies who wouldn't dream of driving their pampered poodles to the groomer in anything less than a convertible BMW. (So-o-o Boca!)

If you're looking for single men with money, this is the place for you. If you're into men with money who don't care what they look like, try rich rancher country — Ocala.

Something You Probably Didn't Know
About This Area

- Florida's film industry is the fastest growing in the nation. In Palm Beach County alone, four films are being made as we go to press.

Best Places to Meet Men

- *The 2 Best Happy Hours in Boca:* **Baci**, 344 Plaza Real in Mizner Park, Boca Raton, 407-362-8500, draws a good crowd of young professionals. Next door is **Max's Grill**, 404 Plaza Real, 407-368-0080, which is equally popular.
- *The Hottest Friday Happy Hour on the Water:* **The Cove**, 1755 S.E. Third Ct., Deerfield Beach, 305-421-9272, is not exactly in Boca Raton — but it's awfully close. And always packed with a 25- to 40-year-old crowd.
- *The Best Sports Bar to Meet the Locals:* **Abbey Road Grill & Sports Emporium**, 710 Linton Blvd., Delray Beach, 407-278-6622. A mixed crowd comes here on Tuesday night to shoot pool and drink beer. A great place to come on game day.
- *The 2 Best "Celebrity" Sports Bars*: **Wilt Chamberlain's**, 8903 W. Glades Rd., Boca Raton, 407-488-8881; and **Pete Rose's Ballpark Cafe**, 8144 W. Glades Rd., Boca Raton, 407-488-7383. Both are a bit more popular with tourists and families than with local singles.
- *The Best Monday Night Crowd:* **Boston's on the Beach**, 40 S. Ocean Blvd., Delray Beach, 407-278-3364. Limbo contests, T-shirt giveaways, and reggae draw a crowd to this restaurant/bar/hotel. The band doesn't start until 10 p.m. — so come late.

- *The Best Ladies Night:* Tuesday at **Croc's Bar and Grill**, 22191 Powerline Rd., Boca Raton, 407-750-8569. Usually packed with young, beeper-carrying professionals. You'll want to get here early, because a line forms around 9 p.m.

- *The Best Body Builder/Boxer Hangout:* **Bay Club**, 2280 N. Federal Hwy., Boynton Beach, 407-734-2726. On Thursday, the club calls itself the "Vatican" and draws the college crowd for alternative night. The older crowd (mid- to late-20s) shows up on Friday for Top-40 music. Live boxing on Wednesday draws a unique mix of amateur fighters, female bodybuilders, and curious onlookers (mostly between ages 20 and 30).

- *The Best Gym to Find Affluent Types:* **Athletic Club**, 1499 Yamato Rd., Boca Raton, 407-241-5088.

- *The Best After-Work-Out Bar:* **Nippers** in Bally's Scandinavian, 21069 Military Trail, Boca Raton, 407-338-4111. Try any weeknight, and you'll find a combination of the just-worked-out, and those looking to meet them. Open every night until 5 a.m

- *The Best Place to Find a Computer Type:* **Hooters**, 2200 W. Glades Rd., Boca Raton, 407-750-9690. IBM's offices are on Yamato Road, but everyone heads to Glades for lunch and happy hour (especially on Fridays).

- *The Best Place to Meet a Young 'Un on Friday Night:* **The Ale House** in Boca, 9244 W. Glades Rd., Boca Raton, 407-487-2989; and the one in Boynton Beach, 2212 N. Congress, Boynton Beach, 407-735-0591, are equally popular. They're open until 4 a.m. and draw a crowd all night.

- *The Best Place to Find a Deadhead:* **Acapulco**

Grill, 201 N.W. First Ave., Boca Raton, 407-394-5449. Wednesday is Dead night, attracting Deadheads from FAU (Florida Atlantic University), and a late-20s to early-30s crowd. Great live bands on weekends.

• *The Best Place to Find a Guy on a Budget:* **Dirty Moe's Oyster Boat**, 395 N.E. Spanish River Blvd., Boca Raton, 407-395-3513. Wednesday is "Nickel Nightmare" night (drafts are a nickel).

• *The Best Place to Meet Literary Singles:* **Barnes & Noble Bookstore**, 1895 N. Congress Ave., Boynton Beach, 407-364-9611, has frequent singles nights — usually the last Thursday of every month.

• *The Best Late Night Spot to Meet Literary Types:* **Liberties Fine Books & Music**, 309 Plaza Real in Mizner Park, Boca Raton, 407-368-1300. Anyone dining out at Mizner Park comes here to browse, mingle, or have coffee afterward. Always crowded and worth a visit.

• *The Best Pick-Up Spot:* **Club Boca**, 7000 W. Palmetto Park Rd., Boca Raton, 407-368-3333. College students get free drinks on Thursdays, so there's always a crowd. Friday is disco night, and Saturday is ladies night (women get free champagne). Things don't get going here on a Saturday night until around 11 p.m.

• *The Best 30+ Pick-Up Spot:* **Wildflower**, 551 E. Palmetto Park Rd., Boca Raton, 407-391-0000. Some women say this place is sleazy, but most agree that this doesn't keep it from being a good place to look for a wealthy guy. Thursdays (ladies night) and weekends are popular.

• *The Best Late Night Pick-up Spot:* **Club Notte**, 5050 Town Center Circle, Boca Raton, 407-393-1221, popular with the over-30 crowd, is open until 4 a.m. on Fridays and Saturdays.

• *The Best Place to Find a Blues Enthusiast:* **The Back Room Blues Lounge**, 16 E. Atlantic Ave., Delray Beach, 407-243-9110.

• *The Best Late-Night Jazz Spot:* **Porterhouse Bar and Grill**, 7050 W. Palmetto Park Rd., Boca Raton, 407-391-6601, attracts a wealthy, professional (20- to 50-year-old) crowd on Thursday night. Don't show up until at least 1 a.m. That's when they begin to migrate here from all the other places that start closing down. Open until 5 a.m.

• *The Best Last Resort:* **Krystals**, 1819 N.W. Second Ave., Boca Raton. This is the only bottle club licensed in Palm Beach County (bring your own booze, and buy the mixers here). A real hot spot during the wee hours. Doors open at 1:30 a.m. and don't close until 8:30 a.m. Membership is about $100 a year, but you can buy a one-night pass for $10. And if you mention this book, owner Stan Prakas says he'll give you a discount.

2. Daytona Beach Area

Along with Panama City, Daytona draws plenty of spring breakers every year. But the thing that really makes Daytona one of the most interesting places in the state to meet men is its race track. Men from all around the country are drawn to **Daytona's International Speedway** (1801 W. International Speedway Blvd., 904-254-2700) for everything from stock car to go-kart racing. If you're into men with fast wheels, this is the place to find them — especially during these special events:

- *Speedweeks.* Late January to mid-February. Begins with the Rolex 24 IMSA race, and ends with the Daytona 500. For information, call 904-253-RACE (7223).
- *Bike Week.* March.
- *Greater Daytona Beach Striking Fish Tournament.* Memorial Day weekend. Weigh-in is at Ponce Inlet. For information, call 904-767-8826.
- *Pepsi 400.* First Saturday in July at the **Daytona International Speedway**. For information, call 904-253-RACE (7223).
- *Biketoberfest/Fall Cycle Scene Championship Cup Series Motorcycle Races.* October at the Daytona International Speedway, and Main Street. For information, call 800-854-1234, or 904-253-RACE (7223).
- *Daytona Beach Fall Speedway Spectacular Car Show and Swap Meet.* Thanksgiving Weekend in Ormond Beach. For information, call 904-677-3454.

2 Things You Probably Didn't Know About Daytona Beach

- While you're here, Miller Beer will give you a free three-minute phone call to anywhere in the country every time you bring in five cans to be recycled.
- You never have to worry about finding a parking place at the beach, because you can park your car on the sand. That's right, people actually drive right onto the beach and sunbathe next to their cars. (An easy way for you to find out what he's driving without asking.)

Best Places to Meet Men

- *The Best Place to Meet a Biker:* **Main Street**,

Daytona Beach. Bike Week is here only once a year, but you can always find leather and motorcycle stuff — and plenty of bikers in the bars. The pier stretches nearly 1/4 mile into the ocean. During any festival, that's the place to be.

• *The Best Place to Meet Surfers:* **Ron Jon's Surf Shop**, 4151 N. Atlantic Ave., Cocoa Beach, 407-799-8888. Open 24 hours a day, this is where the surfers hang out when they're not in the water.

• *The Best Place for Live Blues:* **The Bank**, 701 Main St., Daytona Beach, 904-252-9877. Open only on Friday and Saturday nights.

• *The Best Reggae Bar:* **Kokomos**, 100 N. Atlantic Ave. (Daytona Beach Marriott), Daytona Beach, 904-254-8212. By most accounts, it's worth a visit.

• *The Best Sports Bar:* **The Oyster Pub**, 555 Seabreeze Blvd., Daytona Beach, 904-255-6348. Wear your Yankees cap or Panthers T-shirt and watch big screen TV around the horseshoe bar.

• *The Best Sports Bar for the Young Crowd:* **The Spot**, 176 N. Beach St., Daytona Beach, 904-257-9982. Two-for-one drinks every night.

• *The Best Nightspot for the 25- to 35-Year-Old Set:* **Ocean Deck**, 127 S. Ocean Dr., Daytona Beach, 904-253-5224. The crowd is evenly split between locals and tourists. Live reggae nights are popular, and the place is packed during Bike Week. The best weeknight happy hour is on Thursday.

• *The Best Bar for the Young Crowd:* **The Other Place**, 642 S. Atlantic Ave., Ormond Beach, 904-672-2461. A young (under 25) crowd packs this place, which features live music (heavy metal or hard rock), nine pool tables, and laser disc videos. The best time to go is on "free pool" and "75 cent draft" nights.

- *The Best Place to Meet a Wealthy Skipper:* **Cha Cha Coconuts**, 125 Basin St., Halifax Harbor Marina, Daytona Beach, 904-248-8500. Tropical bar with live music nightly. Open daily. No cover. A real mixed crowd here. (It's brand new, so word is still spreading.)

3. Fort Lauderdale Area

Fort Lauderdale's trendy nightclubs, restaurants, cafes, and shops on Las Olas Blvd. stay open as late as many of the nightspots and attract yuppies from miles around. Once notorious for the antics of college kids on spring break, the city finally tired of scraping them off the sidewalk, and made it clear that they are no longer welcome here. The renovated beach front is now populated with both tourists and locals who enjoy rollerblading along AIA.

Something You Probably Didn't Know About Fort Lauderdale

- The city's popularity as a mecca for spring breakers started during World War II when Ivy Leaguers flocked here because Bermuda (their first choice) was vulnerable to German submarines.

Best Places to Meet Men

- *The Best Place to Meet a Single Stud in Cowboy Boots:* **Desperado**, 2520 S. Miami Rd., Fort Lauderdale, 305-463-2855. Ask him to teach you how to line dance.
- *The Best Sleazy Bar:* **Baja Beach Club**, Oakland Park Blvd. & U.S. 1 in the Coral Ridge Mall, Fort

Lauderdale, 305-561-2432. If it were up to women, this place would be torched. But men flock here, so women are forced to come here to meet them. The big attraction for the men is the nearly naked waitresses that serve up pizza slices and drinks. You'll enjoy watching the boxer-clad bartenders dancing on the tabletops. If you're interested in men who are over 25, stop by during a weekday happy hour.

- *The Best Weekend Bar for the Over-25 Crowd:* **Roxy Nightclub**, 4000 N. Federal Hwy., Fort Lauderdale, 305-565-3555 is a popular weekend pick-up/dance spot. Wednesday is disco night.

- *The Best Place for Young Top-40 Lovers:* **Confetti**, 2660 E. Commercial Blvd., Fort Lauderdale, 305-776-4080. Meet John Travolta wannabes at their Friday night disco parties.

- *The 2 Best Places to Find an Older, More Affluent Crowd:* **September's**, 2975 N. Federal Hwy., Fort Lauderdale, 305-563-4331; and **Yesterday's**, 3001 E. Oakland Park Blvd., Fort Lauderdale, 305-561-4400.

- *The Best Eat-and-Mingle Nightspot:* **Bimini Boat Yard**, 1555 S.E. 17th St., Fort Lauderdale, 305-525-7400. Friday night happy hours attract an affluent, 35-and-over singles crowd.

- *The 2 Best Places on the Beach to Meet a Single Tourist:* **The Elbo Room**, 241 S. Atlantic Blvd., Fort Lauderdale, 305-463-4615, is crammed with sunburned men on weekends; and nearby **Mistral**, 201 S. Atlantic Blvd., Fort Lauderdale, 305-463-4900, is the place to go for happy hour on Friday and for lunch during the week.

- *The Best Nightclub to Meet a Teetotaler:* **Club**

Soda, 5460 N. State Rd. 7, Fort Lauderdale, 305-486-4010. **Club Soda** offers dancing, pool tables, and video games — but no alcohol. Sunday is smoke-free night.

- *The Best Sports Bar to Watch Amateur Boxing on Monday Night*: **Crocco's Sports Bar**, 3339 N. Federal Hwy., Fort Lauderdale, 305-566-2406.
- *The Best Sports Bar to Find Young Guys:* **Calico Jack's**, 801 S. University Dr., Plantation, 305-474-3333. Packed with men on game days.
- *The 3 Best Bars to Meet Locals:* **Parrot Lounge**, 911 Sunrise Ln., Fort Lauderdale, 305-563-1493 draws a youngish (21 to 30) crowd on Friday night, and a down-to-earth neighborhood crowd during the week; **Cafe Blue Fish**, 3134 N.E. Ninth St., Fort Lauderdale, 305-563-3474; and **Village Zoo Cocktail Lounge**, 900 Sunrise Ln., Fort Lauderdale, 305-561-5567 are close by.
- *The 5 Best Happy Hours on Las Olas Boulevard:* **Mangos**, 904 E. Las Olas Blvd., Fort Lauderdale, 305-523-500l; **Mario's East**, 1313 E. Las Olas Blvd., Fort Lauderdale, 305-523-4990; **Arizona 2400**, 2400 E. Las Olas Blvd., Fort Lauderdale, 305-767-9190; **Mark's Las Olas**, 1032 E. Las Olas Blvd., Fort Lauderdale, 305-463-1000; and **O'Hara's Pub**, 722 E. Las Olas Blvd., Fort Lauderdale, 305-524-1764 are popular with professionals who work downtown.
- *The Best Happy Hour With Atmosphere:* **Mai-Kai**, 3599 N. Federal Hwy., Fort Lauderdale, 305-563-3272, has a good turnout on Friday nights. They serve huge tropical drinks, so expect to find some tourists.
- *The Best Place to Meet a Man on a Harley:* Friday nights, after 7:30, in the parking lot of **Fuddrucker's**, 1200 N. Federal Hwy., Fort Lauder-

dale, 305-565-0077.

• *The 3 Best Places to Find a Single, Hip, Jamaican/Caribbean Man:* **Razor's Palace**, 3801 W. Broward Blvd., Plantation, 305-581-0555, is popular on the weekend; **Krystals**, 451 N. State Rd. 7, Plantation, 305-792-4111, is a great spot for dancing on Tuesday and Friday nights; **Memory Lane Cafe**, 4220 State Rd. 7, Lauderdale Lakes, 305-739-5112, draws a big crowd on Saturday night.

• *The Best Place to Score With a Sports Fan:* **Fort Lauderdale Yankee Stadium**, 5301 N.W. 12th Ave., Fort Lauderdale, 305-776-1921 is the winter home of the New York Yankees, and home base for the Fort Lauderdale Strikers soccer team.

• *The Best Place to Find Betting Men:* **Dania Jai-Alai**, 301 E. Dania Beach Blvd., Dania, 305-920-1511.

• *The 3 Best Places to Watch Guys Work Out:* **Gold's Gym**, 1427 E. Commercial Blvd., Fort Lauderdale, 305-491-4653; **Downtown Gym & Fitness Center**, 713 E. Broward Blvd., Fort Lauderdale, 305-462-7669; **Southport Gym**, 1489 S.E. 17th St., Fort Lauderdale, 305-763-9848.

• *The Best Volleyball Action:* The courts behind **Howard Johnson's**, 4660 N. Ocean Dr., Lauderdale-By-the-Sea (just a mile north of Commercial Blvd. on A1A), 305-776-5660.

• *The Best Sports Bar to Find Volleyball Players:* **Sports Page Cafe & Tiki Bar**, Ocean Ranch Hotel, 1110 S. Ocean Dr., Pompano Beach, 305-942-6022, attracts volleyball players (from the courts behind the hotel), as well as beach goers.

• *The 2 Best Coffee Houses:* **The Nocturnal**

Cafe, 110 S.W. Third Ave., Fort Lauderdale, 305-525-9656, where you can sip cappuccino and play kiddie board games; and the **Green Marble Cafe**, 616 E. Atlantic Blvd., Pompano Beach, 305-946-3992, which has poetry readings, good coffee, and earthy guys.

• *The Best Place to Find Literary Types:* **Broward County Main Library**, 100 S. Andrews Ave., Fort Lauderdale, 305-357-7444. Lots of intellectual types come here to do research. The periodical section is an especially good place to meet someone. At lunchtime, check out **Charcuterie**, the restaurant on the second floor (open until 2:30 p.m. on weekdays).

• *The Best Place to Go in the Wee Hours:* **Pickles Night Spot**, 2311 N. Federal Hwy., Pompano Beach, 305-946-2002, stays open until 4 a.m.

• *The Best Last Resort:* **Denny's**, 5000 N. Federal Hwy., Fort Lauderdale, 305-491-1019. Good people watching — and after 2 a.m. on the weekend, you can count on a generous helping of men who didn't get lucky at any of the neighborhood bars.

4. Gainesville

If it weren't for the University of Florida, Gainesville would probably not even be on the map. Everything in this city revolves around the Gators. Though UF scores high academically in engineering, journalism, and accounting, it is better known for being rated as one of the top 10 party schools in the country by *Playboy*. In fact, the social life of UF is so celebrated that Florida high school seniors who aren't accepted here often opt for nearby Santa Fe Community College just to be close to the action.

Any football weekend — especially Homecoming in October — is the best time to visit. That's when the school is packed with loyal alumni who just about guarantee that everyone has a good time.

Something You Probably Didn't Know
About the University of Florida

- It used to be an all-boys school.

Best Places to Meet Men

- *The Best Place to See the Most Men in One Place at One Time:* Any Gators game.
- *The Best Happy Hour:* **Purple Porpoise**, 1728 W. University Ave., Gainesville, 904-376-1667, is a campus dive that's been popular with students and locals forever. Happy hour is from 4 to 7 p.m. The best time to go is during football season — especially after a game.
- *The Best Place to Meet Locals:* **Market Street Pub**, 120 S.W. First Ave., Gainesville, 904-377-2927. This casual place with live music caters to the granola crowd.
- *The 2 Best "Total Meat Markets":* **Kaos**, 201 W. University Ave., Gainesville, 904-374-8002; and its upstairs neighbor **Congo Craig's**, 904-374-8402.
- *The Best Weekend Nightspot:* **T.J. Morrissey's (TJ's)**, 112 S.W. 1st Ave., Gainesville, 904-372-8760.
- *The Best Jock Gym:* The University of Florida's **O'Connell Center**, Gainesville, 904-392-5500, is where you'll find the real campus sports fiends working out.
- *The Best Place for Burrito Lovers:* **Burrito Brothers Taco Co.**, 16 N.W. 13th Ave., Gainesville,

904-378-5948. Try the supreme beef burrito, double-wrapped with tons of sour cream. Open every day from 11 a.m. to 10 p.m.

• *The Best Grunge Dance Club:* **Florida Theatre**, 233 W. University Ave., Gainesville, 904-375-7361. On local band night, beer is $1.75.

• *The Best Grunge Happy Hour:* **Covered Dish**, 210 S.W. 2nd Ave., Gainesville, 904-377-3334. Happy hour is from 2 to 9 p.m. on the patio — with free pizza until 7 p.m. (very popular with budget-conscious students).

• *The Best Place to Find a Cowboy:* **D.J. Chaps**, 108 S. Main St., Gainesville, 904-377-1619. $1 drinks and free dance lessons make Sundays very popular.

• *The Best Place to Find Men Who Like Petite Women:* **Full Circle**, 6 E. University Ave., Gainesville, 904-377-8080. You're supposed to be 5'4" or under to get into **Full Circle**'s "Le Petit" room (of course, you can always duck down). Monday is jazz night, Friday is disco night, and Saturday is alternative/progressive night. **Full Circle** is also open every day for coffee (and general hanging out) from 7 a.m. to 3 a.m. — which is when you catch the locals.

• *The Best Eating Place to Find UF Professors:* **Farah's on the Avenue**, 1120 W. University Ave., Gainesville, 904-378-5179. The profs come in for falafel and a drink during the lunch hour, and come back for Farah's Friday night happy hour. The alums crowd the place during football season because there are TVs all over the place. And everyone else hangs out here Wednesday through Saturday.

• *The Best Place to Find Vegetarians:* **Coney Island**, 210 S.E. First St., Gainesville, 904-372-9288.

Come Friday or Saturday night to graze on veggies and hang out with the hippies.

• *The Best Lunch Spot:* **Joe's Deli**, 1802 W. University Ave., Gainesville, 904-375-5637. Joe has several locations, but this one is the most popular. You'll find hordes of hungry, cash-poor college guys here — especially after a game.

• *The Best Place for Breakfast:* **Bageland**, 1717 N.W. 1st Ave., Gainesville, 904-372-2435. Lots of guys stop here in the morning or between classes.

• *The Best Place to Jog:* Anywhere on campus. You'll run into students, alumni, and professors.

• *The Best Campus Library for General Socializing:* Second floor of **Library East**, Gainesville, 904-392-0326. The cappuccino machine is right downstairs.

• *The Best Campus Library to Meet Greeks:* Fourth floor of the **Marston Science Library**, Gainesville, 904-392-2851.

• *The Best Library to Meet an Aspiring Attorney:* **The UF Law Library**, Gainesville, 904-392-0417.

• *The Best Last Resort:* **Skeeters**, 238 W. University Ave., Gainesville, 904-375-9944. This 24-hour diner has been a late-night tradition for ages. Unfortunately, it lost some of its appeal (and customers) when it recently moved to a location near campus. Still, it's a great place to find collegians munching on big biscuits after a long night of partying.

5. Jacksonville

Everybody in Jacksonville brags about two things: How huge the city is (it's Florida's largest — 841 square miles), and how beautiful the beaches are.

Home of the University of North Florida, Jacksonville is also the home of the PGA Tour's world headquarters, and the International Association of Tennis Professionals. So it's not surprising that the city has so many top-rated golf courses and tennis courts.

Something You Probably Didn't Know About Jacksonville

- President James Monroe called this city a "festering fleshpot" because so many people hung out on the beach in what was then considered to be skimpy clothing.

Best Places to Meet Men

- *The Best Beaches:* Robin Leach calls **Fernandina Beach** on Amelia Island one of the best beaches in the world. It's about 45 minutes from Jacksonville. Park at Peter's Point. In the city, try well-kept **Ponte Vedra Beach**, or popular Jacksonville Beach.
- *The 2 Best Places to Jog:* **Hanna Park**, 500 Wonderwood Dr., Jacksonville, 904-249-4700; and the **University of North Florida Trails**.
- *The Best Gym to Find Professional Men:* The **YMCA** in the lower lobby of the Barnett Center, 50 N. Laura St., Jacksonville, 904-356-9622.
- *The Best Happy Hour for Professionals:* **River City Brewery**, 835 Museum Circle, Jacksonville, 904-398-2299.
- *The 4 Best Places to Find Young Professionals:* **Pete's Bar**, 117 First St., Neptune Beach, 904-249-9158 (the pool tables bring them in); **North Shore Grill**, 363 Atlantic Blvd, Atlantic Beach, 904-246-6633;

Sun Dog Diner, 207 Atlantic Blvd., Neptune Beach, 904-241-8221; **Cafe on the Square**, 1974 San Marco Blvd., near downtown Jacksonville, 904-399-4848.

- *The Best Late Night Place for Young Professionals:* **Ragtime**, 207 Atlantic Blvd., Atlantic Beach, 904-241-7877.

- *The Best Place to Find Affluent Types:* Get a member to take you to the **Ponte Vedra Inn and Club**, 200 Ponte Vedra Blvd., 904-285-1111.

- *The Best Place to Find Rednecks and Yuppies Under the Same Roof:* **Crazy Horse Saloon**, 5800 Phillips Hwy., Jacksonville (a block south of University Blvd.), 904-731-8892. Go for two-step lessons, or try a game of pool.

- *The Best Neighborhood Bar That Draws the Most Diverse Crowd:* **West Inn Lounge**, 3644 St. Johns Ave. (in the Historic Shops of Avondale), Jacksonville, 904-389-1131. It used to be **Monty's** — and it's still known as **Monty's** to locals who have been coming here for 25 years. Attracts a mixed crowd of mostly 25- to 35-year-olds.

- *The 2 Best Apartment Complexes to Find Yuppies:* **Bay Meadows Apartment and Recreation Community**, 7915 Bay Meadows Circle, Jacksonville, 904-739-1013; and **The Polos at the Ponte Vedra**, 125 Great Harbour Way, Jacksonville, 904-285-1431. To take in the "sights," hang out near the pool and tennis courts.

- *The Best Tourist Attraction:* **Anheuser-Busch Brewery**, 111 Busch Dr., Jacksonville, 904-751-8116. Men visiting Jacksonville can't resist the brewery's historic tour and free samples.

- *The Best Place to Find Jocks:* **Jacksonville Veterans Memorial Coliseum**, 1145 E. Adams St.,

Jacksonville, 904-630-3906, hosts NHL exhibition games, college basketball, and wrestling.

• *The Best Place to See the Most Single Men at One Time (beginning in 1995):* **The Gator Bowl**, 1400 E. Duval St., Jacksonville. The stadium was almost completely torn down when the city got its new football team, the Jacksonville Jaguars. But it's on the mend, and when it re-opens, it will be the place to see men by the thousands.

In October, the University of Florida and the University of Georgia football teams do battle here — an annual event that locals refer to as "the world's largest cocktail party." And, come New Year's Eve, the stadium hosts the creatively named "Gator Bowl."

• *The Best Last Resort:* **Masquerade**, 5800 Phillips Hwy., Jacksonville, 904-730-9930.

• *The Best Last Resort for the Over-30 Crowd:* **T-Birds**, 9039 Southside Blvd., Jacksonville, 904-363-3399.

6. The Keys/Key West

Unless you live under a rock, you've probably heard that Ernest Hemingway, Tennessee Williams, Jimmy Buffett, and scores of other creative people made the Florida Keys their home. Today, Robert Redford, Don Johnson, and George Stephanopoulos occasionally hang out at the **Pier House Resort and Caribbean Spa** in Key West, and Jon Bon Jovi and Richie Sambora stop by **Casa Marina** when they're in town.

This is a place that prides itself on eschewing the typical. It is loaded with both straight and gay singles who care little for mainstream status symbols like cars or condos. Many have quit jobs elsewhere and moved to the Keys to follow their dreams. You'll find brokers-turned-fishermen, lawyers-turned-carpenters, and ad men-turned-restauranteurs.

2 Things You Probably Didn't Know About Key West

- In the 1840s, Key West was Florida's richest city — heavily populated by rich, young bachelors.
- Hemingway's second wife, Pauline, put in Key West's first swimming pool, a $20,000 saltwater oval, while he was off covering the Spanish Civil War.

Best Places to Meet Men

- *The Best Bet in the Water:* Sign up for scuba diving lessons. Not only will you learn a fun sport, you'll discover the joys of "buddy breathing."
- *The Best Bet on the Water:* Tons of boats offer snorkeling and dive charters. But to really get to know your "fellow" passengers, and avoid getting lost in the crowd, make sure you sign up for one of the "six-pack" charters (the smaller boats are allowed to carry a maximum of six).
- *The 3 Best Tourist Traps:* **Sloppy Joe's**, 201 Duval St., Key West, 305-294-5717; **Fat Tuesday**, 305 Duval St., Key West, 305-296-9373; and the daily sunset parties on **Mallory Square**.
- *The Best Bar for the Clean-Cut Crowd:* **Jimmy Buffett's Margaritaville Cafe**, 500 Duval St., Key West, 305-292-1435. Good live music, a small dance floor, and guys in unstained T-shirts.
- *The Best Place to Find a Key West Generation Xer:* **Hog's Breath Saloon**, 400 Front St., Key

West, 305-296-4222. Live music and an outdoor atmosphere in the heart of downtown. Popular with young "drop-outs" — guys with degrees in communications who moved down here to work on charter boats.

• *The Best Place to Find a Brit — Behind Or in Front of the Bar:* **Casablanca's at Bogart's**, 900 Duval St., Key West, 305-296-0637. Popular with preppy residents and tourists. Bass Ale on tap.

• *The Best Place to Find a Sailor:* **Schooner Wharf**, 202 Williams St., Key West, 305-292-9520, catches the guys as they come off the water. It's literally nothing but a bar with a tin roof over it. Live music on weekends — great jukebox in between.

• *The Best Place to Find a Local in Key West:* **The Green Parrot**, 601 Whitehead St., Key West, 305-294-6133. Crowded only on Saturday night when there's live music (usually the reggae-jazz-calypso masters The Survivors), **The Parrot** is laid-back and comfortable. Local workmen, politicians, and professionals mingle easily here. During the day, it's a dark oasis off the hot street, and a great place to catch an afternoon game of pool.

• *The Best Tiki Bar:* **Snapper's Waterfront Saloon and Raw Bar** at mile marker 94.5 (ocean side) in Key Largo, 305-852-5956. This place actually has three bars, but the outdoor tiki bar draws a big crowd for its live entertainment and happy hours.

• *The Best Place to Find Harley Riders:* **Caribbean Club** at mile marker 104 (bay side) in Key Largo, 305-451-9970. This waterfront bar attracts a lot of Harley riders on Sundays. It's also popular during the week for happy hour and sunset parties.

• *The Best Place to Stop on Your Way to Key West:* **Holiday Isle Beach Resort** at mile marker 84.5

in Islamorada, 800-327-7070. This 15-acre property houses 13 bars and seven restaurants. The two favorite hangouts are the **Tiki Bar**, which is always packed because of its nightly live music and weekend Polynesian shows; and **Rum Runners**, where you're most likely to meet young tourists. Holiday Isle is also a great place to indulge in water sports (a perfect way to meet a guy) and shopping. The peak season is between December 24th and April 15th.

• *The Best Place to Go Dancing:* **Woody's Restaurant and Saloon** at mile marker 82 (bay side) in Islamorada, 305-664-4335. A family restaurant during the day, this place is hopping at night. "Big Dick and the Extenders," a southern rock and blues band, is the main attraction Tuesday through Sunday. You'll find a mostly 30+ local crowd. Open until 4 a.m.

• *The Best Place to Find an Affluent Gentleman:* Stop by one of the lounges at **The Cheeca Lodge** at mile marker 82 (ocean side) in Islamorada, 800-327-2888. This expensive fishing resort has the only golf course (nine holes) in the Upper Keys. **The Light Tackle Lounge** is a great place to find a wealthy gentleman after a day of fishing or a round of golf.

• *The Best Sunset Party:* **Lorelei Restaurant and Cabana Bar** at mile marker 82 (bay side) in Islamorada, 305-664-2692. This is *the* place to come to for sunset parties. Features live entertainment nightly.

• *The Best Place Last Resort:* **Hog Heaven Sportsbar** at mile marker 85.5 (ocean side) in Islamorada, 305-664-9669. This bar has the usual sportsbar trappings — pool tables, video games — and is popular with the locals. Open until 4 a.m. every day.

7. Miami

Habla español? If not, you'd better learn — because you're in Miami now. Dade County is 29.9 percent Hispanic.

Though Latin America is a major influence here, the city is truly a melting pot — a conglomeration of the most diverse group of people in the state. You'll find a touch of Europe, a smidge of Brooklyn, a dash of Asia, and a generous helping of the Caribbean.

In Miami, excess is best. The typical car cruises down the road showing off the latest model CD player, at least one cellular phone, a sound system capable of shattering glass, and more neon lights than the local pawn shop.

2 Things You Probably Didn't Know About Miami

• The city was born in a pool room. A legal notice in the July 10, 1896 *Miami Metropolis* called all eligible parties to an assembly in a local pool room on July 28 to select officers and organize a government.

• The magnificent palace **Vizcaya** was built by millionaire bachelor James Deering. Today, many South Florida brides dream of holding their weddings here. And it really is a great setting — if you've got some bucks, that is. Just renting the grounds will set you back at least $10,000.

Best Places to Meet Men

• *The Best Place to Find Literary Types:* **Books and Books**, 296 Aragon Ave., Coral Gables, 305-442-4408. The women who work here say most of the interesting men hang out in fiction, but we recommend that

you also try the computer, science, and periodical sections.
- *The Best Downtown Place to Find Literary Types:* **Downtown Book Center**, 247 S.E. First St., Miami, 305-377-9939 — especially during lunch hour.
- *The 2 Best Clubs to Find Cuban Men:* **Club Mystique** in the Miami Airport Hilton, 5101 Blue Lagoon Dr., Miami, 305-265-3900; and **The Firehouse Four**, 1000 S. Miami Ave., Miami, 305-379-1923.
- *The 2 Best Places to Find "Oye Mamita" Types (Partiers and Young Professionals):* **Monty's Raw Bar**, 2550 S. Bayshore Dr., Coconut Grove, 305-858-1431; and **Alcazaba** in the Hyatt Regency Hotel, 50 Alhambra Plaza, Coral Gables, 305-441-1234, on Wednesday, Friday, and Saturday.
- *The 2 Best Happy Hours for Meeting Latino Professionals:* **John Martin's**, 253 Miracle Mile, Miami, 305-445-3777 (on Friday); and **Doc Dammers Restaurant** in the Omni Colonnade Hotel, 180 Aragon Ave., Miami, 305-441-2600.
- *The 2 Best Places on Key Biscayne for Latinos:* **Stefano's Restaurant** (the late night weekend Latin "meat market"), 24 Crandon Blvd., Key Biscayne, 305-361-7007); and **The Highway Lounge**, upstairs at **Linda B Steak House**, 320 Crandon Blvd., Key Biscayne, 305-361-1111.
- *The 6 Best Places to Meet Middle-Aged Latinos With Lots of Money to Spend (But Not Necessarily Any in the Bank):* Friday happy hour at **Victor's Cafe**, 2340 S.W. 32nd Ave., Miami, 305-445-1313; and next door at **Concord Supper Club**, 2301 S.W. 32nd Ave., Miami, 305-441-6974; Friday and Saturday happy hours at **El Cid**, 117 N.W. 42nd Ave., Miami, 305-642-3144; Saturday night at the bar at **Casa**

Juancho, 2436 S.W. Eighth St., Miami, 305-642-2452; late night Saturday at **Swiss Chateau**, 2471 S.W. 32nd Ave., Miami, 305-445-6103; and **Juanito's Centro Vasco**, 3235 S.W. Eighth St., 305-643-9606.

• *The 2 Best Places to Find Single, Hip, Jamaican/Caribbean Men:* **Sunday's on the Bay** (on Sunday), 5420 Crandon Blvd., Key Biscayne, 305-361-6777; and **Stinger Lounge**, 6029 Miramar Pkwy., Miramar, 305-981-0202.

• *The Best Place on Miami Beach to Find Jewish Men:* **The Villa Deli**, 1608 Alton Rd., Miami Beach, 305-672-9122.

• *The Best Place to Find Jewish Men Wearing Dentures:* **Rascal House**, 17190 Collins Ave., Miami Beach, 305-947-4581. Great food!

• *The Best Place to Find Israeli Men:* **Hollywood Midway Kosher Nightclub**, 1828 Harrison St., Hollywood, 305-923-8311. This stylish supper club is closed on Friday night for the Sabbath.

• *The Best Place to Find Health-Conscious, Single Yuppies:* **Unicorn Village Market** in the Waterways, 3565 N.E. 207th St., Aventura, 305-933-1543. Lots of singles who belong to nearby gyms come here to shop after working out.

• *The Best Trap for Single Tourists:* **Hard Rock Cafe** in Bayside Marketplace, 401 Biscayne Blvd., Miami, 305-377-3110, displays some of the chain's best paraphernalia. Attracts lots of tourists, but locals are known to stop by for lunch and on weekend nights.

• *The 4 Best Places to Find Single Men in Coconut Grove:* **Fat Tuesday**, 305-441-2992, and next door neighbor **Cafe Tu Tu Tango**, 305-529-2222, on weekend nights — both in Cocowalk, 3015 Grand Ave., Coconut Grove; **Tavern in the Grove**, 3416 Main

Hwy., Coconut Grove, 305-447-3884; **Señor Frog**, 3008 Grand Ave., Coconut Grove, 305-448-0999 — popular with college guys on Thursdays (live Latin music), and on the weekend.

- *The Best Sports Bar Owned by a Miami Dolphins Quarterback:* **Dan Marino's American Sports Bar & Grill** in Cocowalk, 3015 Grand Ave., Coconut Grove, 305-567-0013, attracts sports enthusiasts and Dolphins fans. Dan Marino (married) is often seen tending bar. Thursday nights are popular. Check out the bar and the back game room (for video junkies).

- *The Best Sports Bar Chain:* **Hooligan's Pub & Oyster Bar** has three locations in Miami — 9555 S. Dixie Hwy., 305-667-9673; 13135 S.W. 89th Pl., 305-252-9155; 15356 N.W. 79th Ct., 305-829-2329.

- *The Best Place to Meet Business Types:* **Hofbrau Pub & Grill**, 172 Giraldo Ave., Coral Gables, 305-442-2730.

- *The 3 Best Lunch Spots Near the Courthouse to Meet Single Professionals:* **Top Hat Cafe** on the ground floor of the Barnett Bank building, 150 W. Flagler St., Miami, 305-381-6337; **Pi's Place** in the Great Western Bank Tower, 100 S.E. Second St., Miami, 305-539-7097; and **The Latin House**, 8 W. Flagler St., Miami, 305-374-7659.

- *The 3 Favorite Hangouts of Brickell Avenue Attorneys:* **The Big Fish**, 55 S.W. Miami Ave. Rd., Miami, 305-372-3725; **Firehouse Four**, 1000 S. Miami Ave., Miami, 305-379-1923; and **Deli Lane Cafe**, 7230 S.W. 59th Ave., Miami, 305-665-0606.

- *The Best Happy Hour to Find Young Professionals on Friday:* **Tobacco Road**, 626 S. Miami Ave., Miami, 305-374-1198, boasts the city's first liquor license.

- *The Best Happy Hour for a Mix of Americans of All Ages:* **Cafe Iguana**, 8505 Mills Dr. in the Town and Country Center, Miami, 305-274-4948. A younger crowd late at night.

- *The Best Place to Find Horny Professionals:* The parking lot of **Miami Gold**, 17450 Biscayne Blvd., North Miami Beach, 305-945-6030 — a provocative nightclub emporium (next door to **La Bare** male revue for ladies) that is a hotbed of hormones on the weekends. Open 3 p.m. to 6 a.m.

- *Another Good Place to Find Horny Professionals:* Any **Hooters** restaurant (more than 30 Florida locations). Men come here for the chicken wings (calorie counters order them "naked" — meaning without breading), and scantily clad waitresses.

- *The Best Gym to Meet a Young Professional:* **Downtown Athletic Club** on the 15th floor of the Southeast Financial Building, 200 S. Biscayne Blvd., Miami, 305-358-9988.

- *The Best Gym to Meet a College Guy:* Any **Gold's Gym** — but especially the one near the FIU South Campus, 1617 S.W. 107th Ave., Miami, 305-553-8878.

- *The Best Gym to Meet a Yuppie:* **Olympia Gym & Fitness Center**, 20355 Biscayne Blvd., Aventura, 305-932-3500.

- *The Best Gym for the Affluent Crowd:* **Biltmore Fitness Center and Spa** in the lower lobby of the Biltmore Hotel, 1200 Anastasia Ave., Miami, 305-445-1926.

- *The Best Gym to Find Latin Men:* **World Gym**, 3737 S.W. Eighth St., Miami, 305-445-5161.

- *The Best Place to Find a Rich Guy:* **Williams Island**, off 183rd St. and Biscayne Blvd. in North Miami Beach. **Willie's Restaurant** (305-937-7854) has a daily happy hour, and **The Island Club** (305-937-7874) is open Thursday through Sunday. Only problem here is that you need to be escorted by a member or resident.

• *The Best Place to Find a Rich Guy That You Can Only Get to By Boat:* **Fisher Island** off the Mac Arthur Causeway, 305-535-6000, offers weekly wine tastings and other social events at **Cafe Tangier**, **The Beach Club**, and **The Golf Grill** during season.

• *The Best Place to See the Most Single Men at One Time:* **Miami Arena**, 701 Arena Blvd., Miami, 305-530-4400, is home to Miami Heat basketball (November to April), University of Miami basketball (November to March), Miami Hooters football (May to July), and Florida Panthers ice hockey (October to April). The men you never meet anywhere else come to these games.

• *Another Good Spot:* **Joe Robbie Stadium**, 2269 N.W. 199th St., Miami, 305-623-6100. The stadium has the Miami Dolphins (August to December, 800-255-3094), the Florida Marlins (April to October, 305-626-7400) — and all their male fans.

8. Naples/Fort Myers

The best way to describe the laid-back Gulf Coast is to imagine Key West and Palm Beach merging into one. You'll find a wide range of friendly, single men here that reflect this interesting blend — everything from the grunge students attending **Edison Community College**, to the transplanted Ivy Leaguers from the Northeast and Midwest, to the wealthy retirees who frequent the prestigious **Pelican Bay Club** in Naples.

Something You Probably Didn't Know About This Area

- Local women say if you're looking for construction workers, you'll find them here, because this place doesn't stop growing. Since 1980, the population of Collier County has doubled.

Best Places to Meet Men

- *The Best (and Only) Nightclub in Naples:* **Club Oasis**, 2023 Davis Blvd., Naples, 813-774-9399, is a hot spot for locals and tourists of all ages. The 10,000 square-foot club features everything from Top-40 to alternative music. Biggest crowd is on weekend nights.

- *The Best 40-Plus Pick-Up Spot:* **Witch's Brew**, 4836 Tamiami Trail, Naples, 813-261-4261. Live music every night but Monday. Popular on the weekend.

- *The Best Weekend Hangouts:* **Vanderbilt Inn on the Gulf**, 11000 Gulf Shore Dr., North Naples, 813-597-3151. (Check out the **Chickee Bar** on the beach for live music and fun — and enjoy sunset happy hours during the week.); or **Fat Tuesday**, 1400 Colonial Blvd., Fort Myers, 813-275-0005.

- *The Best Weekday Bar in Fort Myers:* **Slugger's Sports Bar**, 16440 S. Tamiami Trail, Fort Myers, 813-489-0505. Popular on Tuesday, Thursday, and Saturday nights, when **Slugger's** switches over to **"Club Nouveau,"** a Top-40 dance club, after 9 p.m.

- *The 2 Best Sunday Beach Spots in Fort Myers:* **The Reef**, 2601 Estero Blvd., Fort Myers Beach, 813-463-4181; or **The Bridge**, 708 Fisherman's Wharf, Fort Myers Beach, 813-765-0050.

- *The Best Sunday Night Hangout:* **Naples**

Beach Hotel and Golf Club, 851 Gulf Shore Blvd. N., Naples, 813-261-2222. Sunday nights are packed with a wide assortment of folks that come for the live music beginning at about 5:30 p.m.

• *The Best Dark Spot:* **Rumors**, 4770 S. Cleveland, Fort Myers, 813-275-0023, is an intimate nightclub with Top-40 dance music. Monday is male revue night. (Men are let in after the show.)

• *The Best Local Dance Hangout:* **Zoomerz Sports Bar and Grill**, 4811 S. Cleveland, Fort Myers, 813-936-3877. Popular Monday, Wednesday (ladies night), Friday, and Saturday.

• *The Best Top-40 Dance Club:* **Animations**, 3057 Cleveland, Fort Myers, 813-337-2005, is popular with the 21 to 35 crowd, Wednesday through Saturday. Large, sunken dance floor, computerized light show, and five bars. Theme nights vary from rock to country, so call ahead.

• *The 3 Best Gyms to Find a Single Guy:* **Gold's Gym Fitness Center**, 2151 Trade Center Way, Naples, 813-598-4466; **Body Quest**, 2975 Horseshoe Dr. S., Naples, 813-643-7546; the **YMCA**, 5450 YMCA Rd., Naples, 813-597-3148. Go after 5 p.m. during the week to find professionals who come in after work.

• *The Best Bar for Professionals of All Ages:* **Michael's Cafe**, 2950 Ninth St. N., Naples, 813-434-2550. Features live jazz Wednesday through Saturday during season.

• *The Best Bar for the 30-Plus Affluent Set:* **Nick's on the Water**, 1001 10th Ave. S., Naples, 813-649-7770. Located on Naples Bay, Nick's is the place to be for Friday night happy hour, 4 to 7 p.m.

• *The Best Sunset Cocktail Cruise:* **The Naples Princess**, docked at **Nick's on the Water**, 1001 10th

Ave. S., Naples. For information about cruises, call 813-649-2275.

• *The Best Weekend Club:* **Garrett's** in the Registry Resort, 475 Seagate Dr., Naples, 813-597-3232. This seven-level club is open Friday and Saturday evening, and also hosts various events during the year. If you meet someone here, you can move on to the resort's lobby piano bar, or stroll around the hotel's outdoor boardwalk.

• **The Ritziest Bar: The Ritz Carlton Hotel's** lobby bar, 280 Vanderbilt Beach Rd., Naples, 813-598-3300. You don't have to stay at the resort to have a drink here. Stop by anytime — you'll find an affluent crowd.

• *The Best Spot for Alternative Music:* **The Lizard Cafe**, 1780 Commercial Dr., Naples, 813-775-7765.

• *The Best Local Hangout:* **Captain's Cabin**, 3380 Mercantile Ave., Naples, 813-643-2608. A popular spot with locals of all types, from construction workers who drop by in the afternoon to Philharmonic fans who stop by after a concert. The place has quite a few pool tables, and is frequented by local DJ's who guestplay here. Wednesday and Sunday are ladies nights — but **The Cabin** packs them in on weekends, too. The younger, college-age crowd comes in after 10 p.m.

• *The Best Trendy Bar:* **The Ridgeport Pub**, 5425 Airport Pulling Rd., Naples, 813-591-8422. Features a cozy fireplace, big screen TVs, and a diversified crowd from local service people to business professionals.

• *The Best Cafe:* **Fifth Avenue Cafe**, 625 Fifth Ave. S., Naples, 813-434-9601. Indoor/outdoor cafe with an innovative menu and live music every night except Sunday. A European atmosphere with lots of folks hangin' out listening to tunes and sipping coffee. Most crowded on Saturday night.

• *The Best Bar in a Cafe:* **The Bodega Bar** at the back of the Fifth Avenue Cafe, 625 Fifth Ave. S., Naples, 813-434-9601, attracts men with its pool table and big-screen TV.

• *The Best Sports Bar:* **Sports Page Restaurant and Lounge**, 5310 Shirley St., Naples, 813-597-4001. During football season, this dimly lit bar is packed on Monday night — and several softball teams meet here for drinks after games and after practice. Attracts a mostly 30-plus crowd, from construction workers to affluent professionals.

• *The Best Place to Go to Meet a Gators Fan on Game Day:* **Ralph's Tap and Grill**, 2891 Bayview Dr., Naples, 813-732-6566. You can get to this cozy place by boat. The local chapter of the Gator Club and college students meet here to watch football.

• *The Best Hot-Pink Bar:* **Crazy Flamingo**, 2196 Airport Pulling Rd. S., Naples, 813-793-3800. You can always count on a friendly, casual crowd in this little spot. Everything on their raw bar menu is under $8. Caters to the under-35 crowd.

• *The Best Last Resort:* **Swamp Buggy Lounge**, 428 Ninth St., Naples, 813-262-5555, is a biker bar that attracts a mainstream crowd during the wee hours.

9. Orlando/Winter Park

If you want to meet single men in Orlando, stay away from Walt Disney World. The only males who visit the theme park already have a girlfriend or a wife — or they're still in elementary school. But, for the record, you might be interested to know that one-third of all Florida tourists in 1990 had household incomes of more than $60,000, and Walt Disney World was their number one destination.

Not to worry. If you're looking to meet the locals, there are plenty of places to escape to in Orlando and in Winter Park — an exclusive area 15 minutes from downtown Orlando that is popular with Orlando locals (especially on Thursday nights).

Something You Probably Didn't Know About Orlando

• According to the *Wall Street Journal*, Orlando is an "immaculate" city where the public telephones are sprayed with Lysol weekly.

Best Places to Meet Men

• *The Best Place to Listen to Jimmy Buffett Music:* **Hemingway's** in the Hyatt Regency Grand Cypress, One Grand Cypress Blvd., Orlando, 407-239-1234. You'll think you're in Key West when you see all the Hemingway memorabilia on the walls. Order a "Papa Doble" (supposedly a dacquiri Old Hem, himself, concocted), and listen to Jimmy Buffett tunes.

• *The Best Place to Meet Golfers:* **Edwin Watts Golf Shop**, 7297 Turkey Lake Rd., Orlando, 407-345-8451. This is the self-proclaimed "world's largest retailer of professional golf equipment." A golfer's nirvana.

• *The Best Place to See the Most Men at One Time:* Any Orlando Magic basketball game (October through May) at the **Orlando Arena**, 600 W. Amelia

St., Orlando, 407-849-2000.

• *The Best Disney Happy Hour:* **Laughing Kookaburra** lounge in the Buena Vista Palace, Walt Disney World Village, 1900 Buena Vista Dr., Lake Buena Vista, 407-827-2727. Crammed during happy hour — maybe because of the free snack/meals.

• *The Best Disney Place to Party With the Other Tourists:* **Pleasure Island**, Walt Disney World, Lake Buena Vista, 407-934-7781, is loaded with nightclubs and restaurants, each with a slightly different gimmick. Every night is New Year's Eve, here. And "Where 'ya from?" is the most common pick-up line.

• *The Best Downtown Place to Find Tourists:* **Church Street Station**, 129 W. Church St., Orlando, 407-422-2434, is one big party. Hop from place to place. Enjoy bluegrass at **Apple Annie's**, oldies and Rock-n-Roll at **Orchid Garden**, country western at **Cheyenne Saloon and Opera House**, and dixieland at **Rosie O'Grady's**.

• *The Best Place in Church Street Station to Find Locals:* **Phineas Phogs**, 129 W. Church St., Orlando, 407-422-2434, during Wednesday happy hour.

• *The 2 Best Downtown Happy Hours for Locals:* **Pebbles**, 17 W. Church St., Orlando, 407-839-0892; and **Sloppy Joe's**, 41 W. Church St., Orlando, 407-843-5825.

• *The Best Gym to Meet Men:* **Downtown YMCA**, 433 N. Mills Ave., Orlando, 407-896-6901.

• *The Best Place to Find Irish Men:* **Mulvaney's**, 27 W. Church St., Orlando, 407-872-3296. Hang out at this mellow Irish pub to drink ale and listen to live folk music.

• *The Best Place to Find a Cheap Drunk:* **Wally's**, 1001 N. Mills Ave., Orlando, 407-896-6975, is a package store and bar. Standing room only on weekends.

- *The Best Place to Walk Your Dog to Meet a Man:* Around **Lake Eola**, downtown on Rosalind Avenue, during the week.
- *The Best Place to Buy Groceries and Meet a Professional:* **Publix**, 2015 Edgewater Dr., College Park, 407-872-8691.
- *The Best Place to Buy Sneakers and Meet a Runner:* **Track Shack**, 1322 N. Mills Ave., Orlando, 407-898-1313. This place (which also sponsors a lot of runs) is a giant information center for runners.
- *The 2 Best Alternative Clubs:* **The Edge**, 100 W. Livingston St., Orlando, 407-839-4331, stays open late during the week; **Go Lounge**, in Wall Street Plaza downtown (one block north of Church St. off of Orange Ave.), is a little progressive bar in a garage-like setting that serves beers from all over the world.
- *The Best Place to Meet a Cowboy:* **Rodeo**, 12413 S. Orange Blossom Trail, Orlando, 407-438-1335.
- *The Best Place to Meet a Cowboy and Listen to Live Country Music at the Same Time:* **Sullivan's Entertainment Complex**, 1108 S. Orange Blossom Trail, Orlando, 407-843-2934, is a stompin' ground for all the country western types.
- *The 4 Best Places to Find Locals in Winter Park on Thursday Night:* **Border Cantina**, 329 S. Park Ave., Winter Park, 407-740-7227, is a popular Mexican restaurant where locals come for the $2 Swirls (a frozen margarita/sangria mix); **Fat Tuesday**, 310 S. Park Ave., Winter Park, 407-647-8719, is crowded on Thursday — and even more so on Saturday starting at 10 p.m. when you pay $10 and drink free until 2 a.m.;

Bone Fish Billy's, 118 W. Fairbanks Ave., Winter Park, 407-644-6636, attracts a single crowd on Thursday; **Dexter's**, 200 W. Fairbanks Ave., Winter Park, 407-629-1150, is a popular hangout with live music.

• *The Best Last Resort:* **B-Line Diner**, 9801 International Dr. on the lobby level of the Peabody Hotel, Orlando, 407-352-4000, ext. 4460, is open 24 hours. Loud and fun.

10. Palm Beach/West Palm Beach

When most people hear "Palm Beach County," they think of Palm Beach, notorious playground of the rich and famous. But that's far from the only attraction here. Palm Beach County includes 37 municipalities — everything from the towering skyscrapers of downtown West Palm Beach, to the picturesque shacks of Zora Neale Hurston's beloved Belle Glade, to the 17-acre, 118-room mega-mansion (Mar-a-Lago) built by cereal heiress Marjorie Merriwether Post.

This is a huge, sprawling area — with lots of great places to meet guys. Most of the action is in West Palm.

3 Things You Probably Didn't Know
About Palm Beach County

• John F. Kennedy spent the last weekend of his life here.

• There are more golf courses here — 150 — than in any other county in the United States.

• Palm Beach County has a larger Finnish population (about 12,000) than any place else in the world outside of Stockholm, Sweden, and (of course) Finland.

Best Places to Meet Men

- *The Best Places to Meet the Locals:* **Roxy's**, 319 Clematis St., West Palm Beach, 407-833-1003. Easily considered the "Cheers" of downtown West Palm Beach, this bar attracts a varied crowd. Or, in the north end of the county, try **Jox Sports Club**, 200 N. U.S. 1, Jupiter, 407-744-6600.

- *The Best Place to Meet an Alternative Music Lover:* **Respectable Street Cafe**, 518 Clematis St., West Palm Beach, 407-832-9999. Wednesday is retro/alternative night.

- *The Best Place to Meet a Young 'Un:* **Metropolis**, 114 Narcissus Ave., West Palm Beach, 407-655-3977. The crowd tends to be under 25. Thursday is alternative/ladies night.

- *The Best Place to Meet a Young 'Un on Friday Night:* **Palm Beach Ale House**, 2161 Palm Beach Lakes Blvd., West Palm Beach, 407-683-3777. Open until 4 a.m. on Friday and Saturday.

- *The Best Place to Meet a Beer Connoisseur:* **Lost Weekend**, 115 S. Olive Ave., West Palm Beach, 407-835-8016. There are 120 different kinds of beer on tap here, plus tons of dart boards and pool tables. Expect to meet the 20s crowd at this upscale pool hall that features original artwork on the walls.

- *The Best Place to Meet a Young Heir:* **E.R. Bradley's Saloon**, 111 Bradley Pl., Palm Beach, 407-833-3520, is packed with the young and the (wealthy) restless, especially on Thursday (theme parties), Friday, and Saturday nights. Feast on their buffet with the purchase of two drinks during weekday happy hours (4:30 to 6:30 p.m.).

- *The Best Place to Meet an Heir in a Relaxed Setting:* **Chuck and Harold's**, 207 Royal Poinciana

Way, Palm Beach, 407-659-1440, is casual, but upscale. Come late, because early birds only catch the early bird special (the 50-plus crowd).

• *The Best Place to Meet the Elite:* **Palm Beach Polo & Country Club**, 11809 Polo Club Rd., West Palm Beach, 407-798-7000. If it's good enough for His Highness Prince Charles, it's good enough for you. Watch the regulars play polo daily at 10:30 a.m. (free!). In season (December through April), watch them play high goal polo Sunday at 3 p.m. ($6 to $20).

• *The Best Place to Find Expensive Drinks — and Men Who Can Afford Them:* **Au Bar**, 336 Royal Poinciana Way, Palm Beach, 407-832-4800. $10 cover on Friday and Saturday.

• *The Best Place to Run Into a Kennedy:* **The Colony Hotel**, 155 Hammon Ave., Palm Beach, 407-655-5340.

• *The Best Place to Find Irish Men:* **O'Shea's Pub**, 531 Clematis St., West Palm Beach, 407-833-3865.

• *The Best Place to Eat and Meet:* **Toojay's Original Gourmet Deli**, 313 Royal Poinciana Way, Palm Beach, 407-659-7232. Anyone and everyone comes here — from the wealthiest Palm Beach socialite to her maid. At breakfast, yuppies in business suits sit next to sweaty joggers. Best for breakfast on the weekend or lunch during the week.

• *The Best Coffee House:* **Underground Coffee Works**, 105 Narcissus Ave., West Palm Beach, 407-835-4792. Grunge sits next to jewels in the library or at the bar. Local bands perform nightly.

• *The Best Place to Find Celebs Grocery Shopping:* **Publix**, 265 Sunset Ave., Palm Beach, 407-655-4120. You never know who you're going to run into here. Singles going to Bradley's across the street come here to use the ATM or to cash checks on the weekend. Ricardo Montalban, Lorenzo Lamas, JFK Jr., and Brooke Shields have all been spotted loading up on groceries here. If you're star struck, this is your place.

• *The Best Places to Find a Jazz Enthusiast:* **Narcissus**, 200 Clematis St., West Palm Beach, 407-659-1888; and **The Jazz Showcase**, 905 N. Dixie Hwy., 407-832-1200.

• *The Best Place to Meet a Professional During Lunch:* **Comeau Bar & Grill**, 319 Clematis, West Palm Beach, 407-833-2402. Two blocks from the Palm Beach County Courthouse, this restaurant is a mid-day haven for lawyers, judges, and the downtown crowd.

• *The Best Happy Hour on the Water:* **Bimini Bay**, 104 Clematis St., West Palm Beach, 407-833-9554. Features an outdoor patio bar over-looking the Intracoastal Waterway. Attracts a diverse crowd of professionals from downtown West Palm Beach.

• *The Best Place to Meet a Professional Baseball Player During Spring Training:* **Club Safari**, 4000 RCA Blvd., Palm Beach Gardens, 407-622-7024.

• *The Best Place to Meet a Fisherman or Boating Enthusiast on Singer Island:* **The Sailfish Marina**, 90 Lake Dr., Singer Island, 407-844-1724. Features an art show on the dock called "Sunset Celebration" on Thursday nights.

• *The Best Places to Meet Men on Singer Island After a Day at the Beach:* **Greenhouse**, 2401 N. Ocean Ave., Singer Island, 407-845-1333, which features a beachfront patio/deck and indoor restaurant and bar; and **Oceans Eleven North**, 2603 N. Ocean Ave., Singer Island, 407-840-1812, which stays open until 5 a.m. every night of the week.

11. Panama City/Pensacola

People in the Panhandle are real southerners —
meaning they are some of the nicest and most helpful
people you'll meet anywhere in Florida. And it's very
easy to meet men here, especially if you're young and
you like military men. Pensacola is home to the 10,000
sailors stationed at the U.S. Naval Air Station and
the pilots stationed at Eglin Air Force Base, halfway
between Pensacola and Panama City.

Panama City — also known as the Redneck
Riviera, or the poor man's Palm Beach — is a hotbed of activity during spring and summer (late February through Labor Day Weekend) when people flock
here to mingle with vacationing college students and
other beachgoers. But it practically shuts down in
winter.

2 Things You Probably Didn't Know
About the Panhandle

• Pensacola was the home of Florida's first millionaire, William Danton, who made his fortune in the
late 18th century.

• Bar owners say 1994 drew the biggest spring
break crowd in Panama City's history — close to half a
million people over a seven-week period.

Best Places to Meet Men

• *The Best Place to Meet Someone:* The Panama
City beach. The biggest attraction is also the best meeting grounds — 27 miles of gorgeous beach and wild clubs.

• *The 2 Best Bars to Find a Mix of College Students, Military Men, and Beachgoers:* **Spinnaker**,
8795 Thomas Dr., Panama City Beach, 904-234-7882;

and next door at **Club Le Vela**, 8813 Thomas Dr.,
Panama City Beach, 904-234-3866. Both bars attract
a young crowd in the spring and summer.

* *The 4 Best Places to Meet the Panama City
Locals:* **Schooner's**, 5121 Gulf Dr., Panama City Beach,
904-235-9074; **Salty's Beach Bar**, 11073 Front Beach
Rd., Panama City Beach, 904-234-1913; **Breakers**,
12627 Front Beach Rd., Panama City Beach, 904-234-
6060; and **Pineapple Willie's Lounge**, 9900 Beach
Blvd., Panama City, 904-235-0928 attract the 25-to-
50 crowd. Locals are addicted to the good live music
and dancing offered by all these clubs. When you're in
town, find out which place is hosting the best band.
That's the place to be.

* *The 2 Best Places to Go in Panama City in
the Winter:* If you happen to be in Panama City during
the winter (not recommended), try **Thunderbird's
Nightcub**, 4300 W. Highway 98, Panama City, 904-
785-7444; or **No Name Bar**, 5555 W. Highway 98,
Panama City, 904-763-9153.

* *The 4 Best Nightspots in Seville Quarter:*
Seville Quarter, 130 E. Government St. in the Seville
Historic District of Pensacola, 904-434-6211, is home
to seven bars. The best are **Phineas Phoggs** on Monday for nickel beer night, **Rosey O'Grady's** on Thursday night for dancing, **End of the Alley** patio bar for
live music, and **Palace Oyster Bar** for raw oysters.

* *The Best Nightspot Outside the Quarter:* **Rum
Runner**, 500 S. Palafox St., Pensacola, 904-433-9295.
A good weekend spot that draws a younger crowd.

* *The Best Place to Find a Cowboy:* **Roper's**,
5060 Bayou Blvd. in the parking lot of Cordova Mall,
Pensacola, 904-494-1600.

* *The 2 Best Friday Happy Hours:* **Ye Olde**

Beef and Ale, 600 S. Barracks St., Pensacola, 904-435-9719; and its neighbor upstairs, **The Yacht Restaurant**, 600 S. Barracks St., Pensacola, 904-432-3707, both attract a professional crowd.

- *The Best Beach Bar in Pensacola:* **Flounder's Chowder and Ale House**, 800 Quietwater Beach Rd., Pensacola Beach, 904-932-2003. Jimmy Buffett tunes on Sunday. Reggae during the week.
- *The Best Place to Find Men After a Day at the Beach:* **The Dock**, 4 Casino Beach Boardwalk, Pensacola Beach, 904-934-3314. Sunday is rum-and-reggae day. Classic rock during the week.
- *The Best Beach Bar to Meet a Local:* **Sandshaker**, 731 Pensacola Beach Blvd., Pensacola Beach, 904-932-2211, is popular with the locals on the weekend.
- *The Best Place to Jog:* On Pensacola Beach, and on the nature trail at the University of West Florida, 11000 University Pkwy., Pensacola, 904-474-2000.
- *The 3 Best Gyms to Meet Men:* **Gold's Gym**, 5007 N. Davis Hwy., Pensacola, 904-484-0849; **Pensacola Health Club**, 5404 Sun Valley Dr., Pensacola, 904-433-5877; **Pensacola Downtown Gym and Fitness Center**, 801 E. Cervantes St., Pensacola, 904-438-0111.
- *The Best Place to Meet a Guy on a Harley:* **Butterball Cack's Saloon**, 4133 Barrancas Ave., Pensacola, 904-453-8127 — and the tattoo parlor in the same complex.
- *The Best "Men Are Pigs Night":* Wednesday at **Coconuts Comedy Club**, 7200 Plantation Rd., Pensacola, 904-484-6887. Guys from both the Air Force and Navy bases hang out here — especially on Wednesday when the club draws the ladies with dis-

counted drinks.

- *The Best Place to Meet a Naval Aviator:* **McGuire's Irish Pub**, 600 E. Gregory St., 904-433-6789. Their slogan is "Feasting, Imbibery, and Debauchery," and as their recording says, "If you don't like crowds, don't show up."
- *The Best Place to Find the Most Diverse Crowd:* **Flora-Bama**, 17401 Perdido Key Dr., Pensacola, 904-492-0611. Right on the border between Florida and Alabama, this place draws all types — from your $5 man to your $5 million man. Jimmy Buffett plays here when he's in town.
- *A Must See:* **Trader John's Tavern**, 511 S. Palafox, Pensacola, 904-433-7113. A Navy memorabilia bar, and home to the largest Blue Angel collection in the world. Prince Andrew even stopped by when he was in town. (The inside joke here is that you'll never find the owner wearing a matching pair of socks.)

12. Sarasota

Legend has it that Spanish explorer Hernando De Soto had a beautiful daughter named Sara Sota. An Indian prince fell madly in love with her and allowed himself to be taken prisoner by the Spaniards just so he could be near her. When he got sick, Sara nursed him back to health, but caught the bug herself and died.

Today, Sarasota is known as one of the best places in the state to find a single man with money. And though the city has the highest woman-to-man ratio in the country (100 single women to every 65 men), the situation really isn't too bad for young husband hunters, because most of those single women are over 65.

Something You Probably Didn't Know About Sarasota

- This is the home of Florida's first golf course, a four-holer built by Colonel J. Hamilton Gillespie in 1886.

Best Places to Meet Men

- *The Best Place to Jog:* **Siesta Beach** on Siesta Key. You'll find lots of soft skin and hard bodies.
- *The Best Jock Watching:* March and April at the **Ed Smith Stadium**, 2700 12th St., east of downtown Sarasota, 813-954-4101, when the Chicago White Sox practice.
- *The Best Place to Find Literary Types:* **Main Bookshop**, 1962 Main St., Sarasota, 813-366-7653.
- *The Best Happy Hour:* **Sarasota Brewing Company**, 6607 Gateway Ave., Sarasota, 813-925-2337.
- *The 2 Best Places to Find Laid-Back Types:* **Limerick Junction Pub**, 1296 First St., Sarasota, 813-366-6366, features Irish beer, poetry readings, and ambiance; and you'll find a similar crowd at the **Monterey Deli and Pub**, 1468 Main St., Sarasota, 813-366-9788.
- *The Best Work-Week Hangout:* **Gecko's Restaurant and Pub**, 4870 Tamiami Trail South, Sarasota, 813-923-8896. Popular singles scene during the week. Mostly young business professionals with both blue and white collars.
- *The 2 Best Pick-Up Spots:* **In Extremis**, 204 Sarasota Quay in the Quay Plaza, Sarasota, 813-954-2008, for a younger crowd (Wednesday is ladies night); **The Beach Club**, 5151 Ocean Blvd., Siesta Key, 813-

349-6311, attracts a young crowd on the weekend. (This is not only a great place to check out men, it's also a great place to listen to music.)

• *The Best Place to Find the Locals:* **Livingston's Billiards**, 7113 S. Tamiami Trail, Sarasota, 813-925-7665.

• *The Best Place in Nearby Venice Beach:* **Sharky's**, 1600 S. Harbor Dr., Casperson Beach, near the fishing pier in Venice, 813-488-1456.

• *The Best Place for Late Night Dancing:* **Funkshun**, 6543 Gateway Ave., Sarasota, 813-924-4451.

• *The Best Last Resort:* **Sarasota Bottle Club**, 2264 Gulf Gate Dr., Sarasota, 813-921-6764.

13. South Beach

Welcome to the trendiest (South Beachers prefer "hippest") place in Florida, where you'll find attitudes by the thousands — all dressed in black.

Looking "in" is key on South Beach. If you look like money, a model, or the friend of a model with money, life is sweet. Some SoBe doormen think they're in Manhattan, so they hand-pick the chic to enter their clubs. Knowing the night's password or the club owner's name can get you in. If not, a handshake with a $5, $10, or $20 bill works just as well. Try getting friendly with the men in line with you — if they bribe the doorman, you can slip in with them. Or, if you don't mind being treated like a cow at a cattle auction, just hang out in line until you finally catch the doorman's eye.

A few words of warning: Be cautious of clubs with

lines of men in front of them. Gay clubs (Paragon, Warsaw Ballroom, Twist, Snap, and Kremlin, for example) are popular on the beach. So if you're looking for someone to father your children — look elsewhere. Also, keep in mind that on South Beach, the clubs change as often as the fashions. What was hot last week, may not even be there this week. So call before you go.

One last thing you need to know — the best times to meet men on South Beach are during the day on Saturday or Sunday, in the evening during the week, and after midnight on Friday night. (11 p.m. is considered early.)

5 Things You Probably Didn't Know About South Beach

- Frank Sinatra, a one-time South Beach regular, filmed "A Hole in the Head" in 1959 in the Cardozo Hotel.

- Desi Arnaz once tried out a new dance on Española Way (between Washington and Drexel Avenues) — a favorite spot with film crews because of its Disney-esque vision of peach Mediterranean buildings framed by palm trees. Today, Desi's dance is called the rhumba.

- Al "Scarface" Capone bought a two-story house in Miami Beach in 1928 and lived there until he died in 1947.

- An ad for Calvin Klein's Obsession started everyone running back to Miami's South Beach when, in 1988, photographer Bruce Weber shot a pair of bare buns on an Art Deco rooftop.

- In this land of deco decadence, it's not unusual to spot famous celebrities like Madonna (who owns a home in Miami), singer Gloria Estefan (owner of **Lario's**

on the Beach restaurant), and designer Gianni Versace, whose luxurious home sits on Ocean Drive.

Best Places to Meet Men

- *The Best Way to Meet a Man on South Beach:* Hang out on Ocean Drive between 5th and 15th Streets. On the weekend, Ocean Drive is packed with hard-bodies rollerblading, playing volleyball, or just walking up and down the beach flexing their biceps.

- *The Best Beach:* Find a beach with a volleyball net, and you'll find gorgeous bodies. There are lots of popular spots to tan (with and without a top) in the area between 8th and 10th Streets.

- *The Best Place to Buy a Condom:* **Condomania**, 760 Washington Ave., South Beach, 305-531-7872. Seventy percent of the condoms here are usable — the rest are novelties. Open until midnight on Friday and Saturday, this place has everything from the Small Pecker Condom ("to cover the little things in life"), to the Condom Patch ("more bangs for the buck"), to the Stealth Condom ("they'll never see you coming").

- *The 4 Best Places to Find a Man With Fashion Flair, an Attitude, Lots of Cash, Connections — or Some Combination Thereof:* **Les Bains**, 753 Washington Ave., South Beach, 305-532-8768 during the week (closed in summer); **Van Dome**, 1532 Washington Ave., South Beach, 305-534-4288; **Lua**, 409 Espanola Way, South Beach, 305-534-0061; **Bash**, 655 Washington Ave., South Beach, 305-538-2274.

- *The Best Al Fresco Hot Spot:* **Amnesia**, 136 Collins Ave., South Beach, 305-531-5535. When you drive by, **Amnesia** looks like an indoor club, but it's not — so skip it if it's raining. But when the sun shines, it's a great place to find affluent men.

- *The 2 Best Places to Find Men Who Don't Mind Hefty Cover Charges:* **Glam Slam** (Prince's club), 1235 Washington Ave., South Beach, 305-672-2770; Dune (used to be **Le Loft**), 1439 Washington Ave., South Beach, 305-672-7111.
- *The Best Place to Find Young Professionals:* Friday night at **The Strand**, 671 Washington Ave., South Beach, 305-532-2340.
- *The Best Place to Find Latinos:* The bar at **Mezzanotte** restaurant, 1200 Washington Ave., South Beach, 305-673-4343, has been popular for years. It's not unusual to see people dancing on the tables after 11 p.m.
- *The Best Latino Dance Club:* **Coco Bongo** (formerly **Club One**), 1045 Fifth St., South Beach, 305-534-4999.
- *The Best Club to Find Young Latino Professionals:* Friday night at **Nick's Miami Beach**, 300 Alton Rd., South Beach, 305-673-3444. Men have to be 23 to get in — 21 for women.
- *The Best Place to Find an Out-of-Towner:* **The Clevelander** hotel, 1020 Ocean Dr., South Beach, 305-531-3485. A mostly young crowd on the weekend. They dance outdoors to live music and hang out around the pool, lobby, and pink-neon-rimmed bar.
- *The Best Place to Find Affluent Men:* **Joe's Stone Crab**, 227 Biscayne St., South Beach, 305-673-0365, in season (October 15 through May 15). Sit at the bar and be on the lookout for the guys who bribe the maitre'd for a good seat. They're the ones with money.
- *The 2 Best Places to Find Attitude-Free Men:* **Stephen Talkhouse**, 616 Collins Ave., South Beach, 305-531-7557; and **Rose's Bar & Music Lounge**, 754 Washington Ave., South Beach, 305-532-0228.

- *The Best Place to Find Young Bee Gees Fans:* Sunday night disco parties at the **Cameo Theater**, 1445 Washington Ave., South Beach, 305-532-0922.
- *The Best Eclectic Club:* **The Spot**, 218 Española Way, South Beach, 305-532-1682, is next door to a Harley shop, so you'll always find bikers hanging out on the street. And after midnight, **The Spot** attracts all sorts of men — especially those who aren't self-conscious about dancing alone.
- *The Best Place to Find Literary Types:* **Books & Books**, 933 Lincoln Rd., South Beach, 305-532-3222.
- *The Best Place to Find a Man Grocery Shopping:* **Publix**, 1041 Dade Blvd., South Beach, 305-538-7250. Open until 11 p.m.
- *The Best Place for Late-Night Grocery Shopping:* **Stephan's Gourmet Market**, 1430 Washington Ave., South Beach, 305-674-1760, is open until 2 a.m. Friday and Saturday.
- *The Best Grocery for Men With Taste and Dinero:* **Epicure Market**, 1656 Alton Rd., South Beach, 305-672-1861. You'll find quality, not quantity.
- *The Best Last Resort:* **News Cafe**, 800 Ocean Dr., South Beach, 305-531-0392. Its location at the corner of 8th and Ocean makes it the perfect people-watching spot. Sooner or later, everyone walks by here. **News Cafe** is also a popular eating spot — crowded day and night.

14. Tallahassee

Prince Achilles Murat of Naples, nephew of Napoleon Bonaparte and son of the King of Naples, came to young Tallahassee to seek his fortune in the late 1820s. There he met Catherine Willis Dangerfield Gray, the great grand-niece of George Washington. The happy couple were issued the 8th marriage license in Leon County.

Most people, however, don't think of this tender love story when they think "Tallahassee." Located exactly halfway between Saint Augustine (the state's oldest city) and Pensacola, the city is best known for being the state capital — and the home of Florida State University (FSU) and Florida A & M University. The wildest men in this conservative city belong either to the state legislature, or college fraternities.

Something You Probably Didn't Know About FSU

• FSU's football team is aptly named. "Seminole" is a corruption of the Greek "ishtisemoli," meaning "wild man."

Best Places to Meet Men

• *The Best Barhopping:* Doing the "Tennessee Waltz" in T-town — meaning hopping from bar to bar on Tennessee Street. The Strip is especially popular on Thursdays.

• *4 of the Hottest Spots on the Strip:* **Poor Paul's Poorhouse**, 618-1/2 W. Tennessee St., Tallahassee, 904-222-2978; **Big Daddy's Draft House**, 654 W. Tennessee St., Tallahassee, 904-561-6449; **Bullwinkles Tavern**, 620 W. Tennessee St., Tallahassee, 904-224-0651 (especially crowded on Wednesday, Thursday, and Saturday); **Metropolis**, 666-1 W. Tennessee St., Tallahassee, 904-681-9927 (busy on

Sunday); **Ken's Tavern**, 656 W. Tennessee St., Tallahassee, 904-599-9062 (popular with locals during the day, and college students at night), has been around for 28 years.

• *The 2 Best Sports Bars on the Strip:* **A.J. Sports Bar**, 1800 W. Tennessee St., Tallahassee, 904-681-0731, is popular for hospitality night on Wednesday; on Friday, try **Doc's Sports Bar**, 1921 W. Tennessee St., Tallahassee, 904-224-5946.

• *The Best Place to Meet a Liberal:* **Yianni's Cafe**, 646 W. Tennessee St., Tallahassee, 904-681-9565.

• *The Best Place for Country Western Two-Stepping:* **The Riverfront Saloon**, 9330 W. Tennessee St., Tallahassee, 904-575-1100, on Thursday.

• *The Best Club Off Tennessee Street:* **The Moon**, 1105 E. Lafayette St., Tallahassee, 904-222-6666. Drinks and dancing — but be sure to call ahead to make sure you don't wind up there on teen night.

• *The Best Place to Find Politicians After Hours:* **Clyde's and Costello's**, 210 S. Adams St. in downtown Tallahassee, 904-224-2173. Popular all year round, but especially when Congress is in session. During these 90 days beginning in February, you'll find all sorts of politicos hanging out here. (And at least one lobbyist is known to have run a $15,000 tab here.)

• *2 Other Downtown Spots to Check Out:* **Fat Tuesday**, 101 S. Adams in the Holiday Inn Capitol Plaza, Tallahassee, 904-224-5000; and **Club Park Avenue**, 115 E. Park Ave., Tallahassee, 904-599-9143.

• *The Best Place to Jog:* **Tallahassee-Saint**

Mark's Historic Railroad Trail. The entrance is on Fla. 363 just south of Tallahassee. (People also bicycle and Rollerblade here.)

- *The Best Jock Gym:* **Legend Fitness Club**, 2415 N. Monroe, Tallahassee, 904-386-4000.

- *The 2 Best Places to See the Most Single Men at One Time:* **Leon County Civic Center**, 505 W. Pensacola St., Tallahassee, 904-487-1691, hosts the city's first minor league hockey team, the Tallahassee Tigersharks. Or watch the Florida State Seminoles play at **Dow Campbell Stadium**.

- *The Best Place to Buy a Condom:* **Condomology**, 522 W. Gaines St., Tallahassee, 904-224-7827. New on the shelves is the Bill Clinton Bubba Rubba ("even the Secret Service can't provide this kind of protection").

15. Tampa/St. Pete

Tampa Bay is also known as the Sun Coast. The area is home to the University of South Florida (USF)—also known as Long Island South since so many New Yorkers wind up here. Tampa is also home to the number-one tourist trap on the west coast — Busch Gardens (a place to stay away from if you're looking for single men) — and home of famous bachelor, and two-time Wimbledon champ, Pete Sampras.

Something You Probably Didn't Know About Tampa Bay

- Teddy Roosevelt drilled his Rough Riders in the backyard of the Tampa Bay Hotel.

Best Places to Meet Men

• *The Best Place to See the Most Men at One Time:* **Tampa Bay Stadium**, 4201 Dale Mabry Hwy., Tampa, 813-872-7977, is a home away from home for Tampa men. They come for motorcycle races and tractor pulls, as well as Bucs games.

• *The Best Place to Meet a Hockey Fan:* At a Tampa Bay Lightning game at the **ThunderDome**, 16th St. and 1st Ave. S., St. Petersburg, 813-825-3120. Season runs October through April.

• *The Best Place to Meet Men During Lunch Hour:* The open-air **Franklin Street Mall** in downtown Tampa.

• *The Best Place to Find Horny Men:* At the world-famous **Mons Venus** strip club, 2040 Dale Mabry Hwy., 813-875-2762. The big attraction here (for the men) is that there's a little more contact allowed than at your average joint.

• *The Best Place to Meet Men Who Jog or Rollerblade:* **Bayshore Boulevard** right after work during the week.

• *The Best Church to Meet Single Men:* Tampa women recommend **Palma Ceia Presbyterian Church**, 3501 San Jose, Tampa, 813-253-6047.

• *The Best Annual Festivity:* **Gasparilla** in February — Tampa's version of Mardi Gras — features pirates, parades, and music. Lots of society types here. For information, call 800-826-8358, ext. 34.

• *The Best Area to Find Yuppie Nightspots:* **Ybor City**, just east of downtown, is home to many great clubs. Try **Blues Ship**, 1910 E. Seventh Ave., Ybor City, 813-248-6097; **The Castle**, 2004 16th St., Ybor City, 813-247-7547; **Ritz Theater**, 1503 E. Seventh Ave., Ybor City, 813-247-3319; **Carmine's**, 1802 E. Seventh Ave.,

Ybor City, 813-248-3834; and **Harpo's**, 1805 E. Seventh Ave., Ybor City, 813-248-4814.

- *The Best Happy Hour in Ybor City:* **Frankie's Patio**, 1920 E. Seventh Ave., Ybor City, 813-248-3337.
- *The Best Concert Series:* **Old Hyde Park** outdoor concerts on Swann & Dakota near Bayshore Boulevard in Tampa. For information, call 813-251-3500.
- *The Best Place to Meet an Alternative Music Lover:* **911**, 911 Franklin N., Tampa, 813-224-0911.
- *The Best Area for Affluent Men:* **Old Hyde Park**, 712 S. Oregon Ave., is this city's version of Miami Beach's Bal Harbor, Palm Beach's Worth Avenue, or Boca Raton's Mizner Park. Many of the homes here are historic landmarks.
- *The 2 Best Places to Try in Old Hyde Park:* **Cactus Club**, 1601 Snow Ave., Old Hyde Park, 813-251-4089, has a good happy hour; and **Selenas**, 1623 Snow Ave., Old Hyde Park, 813-251-2116, attracts affluent, middle-aged, single men on Friday night.
- *The Best Place to Meet an Attorney:* **Four Green Fields**, 205 W. Platt, Tampa, 813-254-4444, is nicknamed "four hundred green lawyers" because so many attorneys hang out here during happy hour.
- *The Best Place to Find a Young Professional Type:* **Cold Storage Cafe**, 301 N. Florida St., Tampa, 813-221-4591. Great happy hour on Friday!
- *The Best Pick-Up Spot:* **Yucatan Liquor Stand**, 4811 W. Cypress St., Tampa, 813-289-8454. Ask about their volleyball tournament.
- *The Best Place to Pick Up a Guy Who Likes to Dance:* **Stingers**, 11921 N. Dale Mabry Hwy., Tampa, 813-968-1515.
- *The Best Place to Meet a Blind Date:* **Joffrey's Coffee and Tea Company**, 1628 W. Snow Circle in

Old Hyde Park Village, 813-251-3315. If nothing else, at least you'll enjoy the coffee.

- *The 3 Best Gyms:* **Harbour Island Athletic Club**, 900 S. Harbour Island, Tampa, 813-229-5062; downtown **YMCA**, 104 S. Franklin St., Tampa, 813-229-1305; **Bally's**, 4002 Gandy Blvd., Tampa, 813-831-5996.
- *The Best Place to Meet Someone in Line:* **Mel's Hot Dogs**, 4136 E. Busch Blvd., Tampa, 813-985-8000. Strike up a conversation with him about the hot dog cartoons and fan mail on the walls.
- *The Best Place to Meet a Yachtsman:* **Davis Island Yacht Club**, 1315 Severn, Tampa, 813-251-1158. Lots of affluent types come here for the Thursday night races in the spring and summer.
- *The Best Grocery Store to Meet Men:* **Kash 'n Karry**, 2100 W. Swann Ave., Hyde Park, 813-254-6800. Open 24 hours.
- *The Best Burger Joint:* **Jimmy Mac's**, 113 S. Armenia Ave., Tampa, 813-879-0591. Try squeezing into the bar at lunch or dinner. Happy hour is yuppy hour.
- *The Best Place to Eat and Meet:* **Kojak**, 2808 Gandy Blvd., Tampa, 813-837-3774. The office crowd mixes with soldiers from the military base to chow down on pork ribs and pork sandwiches. (Not a good place to meet a vegetarian.)
- *The Best Place to Find a Guy Who Likes Alligator Sandwiches and Alligator Black Bean Chili:* **Skipper's Smokehouse and Oyster Bar**, 910 Skipper Rd., Tampa, 813-971-0666. During lunch, look for USF profs. At night, join the bare-foot crowd, outside, dancing to reggae and live blues, and drinking dirt-cheap beer.

- *The Best Place for Intellectual Conversation:* **Ovo Cafe**, 1901 E. Seventh Ave., Ybor City, 813-248-6979, is a great place to meet someone. Come after midnight, and chat over cappuccino, apple pie, or waffles.
- *The Best Beachfront Bar/Restaurant:* **The Hurricane**, 807 Gulf Way, St. Petersburg Beach, 813-360-9558. This seafood restaurant features live jazz and a roof-top bar with music, dancing, and a great view of the beach.
- *The Best Last Resorts:* **Chatterbox**, 709 S. Howard Ave., Tampa, 813-251-3628, is open until 3 a.m. Wednesday through Saturday. Also worth a try is **The Hideaway**, across the street at 720 S. Howard Ave., Tampa, 813-254-5540.

Singles/Networking Groups

Very few of these groups operate out of a real office complete with a secretary to answer the phone. When you call, you're much more likely to get a member's home answering machine, or his/her daytime work phone. Don't think you've dialed a wrong number. Just say why you're calling — and you'll get through to the right person.

Statewide Groups & Organizations

• *American Jewish Singles.* Dance and cocktail parties in Dade, Broward, and Palm Beach Counties for Jewish singles in their 30s to 50s; 305-720-8994.
• *American Singles Association.* Business card exchanges, charity fundraisers, cruises, sports, and dinner parties for Broward and Palm Beach County professionals in their late 20s to mid-60s.; 305-929-1200.
• *American Singles Party Network.* Two Jewish singles groups and one non-denominational group; 407-393-8895 or 407-393-9193.
• *Ann Rotman's Tres Chic Events.* Parties at bars, comedy clubs, etc. for Jewish singles; 305-458-9914.
• *Barnes & Noble Bookstores.* Many stores schedule monthly singles nights featuring lectures and various literary

events. Contact the store in your area for information.

• *Bayberry Travel/Carlson Travel Network.* Singles and networking tours (mostly on weekends) and tours to Europe, Club Med, and various Florida destinations; 305-935-5560 or 800-933-5560 (ask for Shuly Pfeffer).

• *Christian Singles Network.* Support groups, dating services, and social events; 305-476-5606. $25 annual membership fee.

• *Christian Singles Smoke-Free Dances.* Held in Broward and Palm Beach Counties; 305-755-7727. Dance lessons available.

• *Cystic Fibrosis Fundraisers.* Sponsor annual bachelor/bachelorette auctions (featuring the area's "finest" singles) and other networking events in Boca Raton, Miami, and Fort Lauderdale; 305-947-4243 (Miami) or 305 426-3918 (Fort Lauderdale and Boca Raton).

• *Dinner Theaters, Comedy Plays, and Murder Mystery Parties for Singles.* Call Cathy Rollins at 407-368-5252 or 305-971-7555.

• *Faces.* Parties for Jewish singles 21 to 45; 305-932-4192.

• *Florida Federation of Young Republicans.* Call the chapter in your area for information.

• *Florida Junior Chamber of Commerce (Jaycees).* Leadership training, community service, social events for individuals 21 to 40. Call the chapter service center at 813-688-5481 for information about the Jaycees in your area.

• *Florida Young Republicans.* A great political and social group. For information about the chapter nearest you, contact the Republican Party of Florida at 904-222-7920.

• *Golf Lovers U.S.A.* A unique golf league for singles; 407-995-8823. All levels, all ages welcome.

• *Guys and Dolls Singles.* Bowling parties in Broward and Palm Beach Counties for singles 35 to 50; call Dom at 305-722-9814.

• *Jewish Community Centers.* Sponsor many singles groups and events. Contact the JCC in your area.

• *Jewish Young Singles.* Weekly dances and social events in Dade, Broward, and Palm Beach Counties for singles 21 to 45 and 35 to 55; 305-932-4192. No membership fee.

• *Let's Meet at the Movies.* Members of this group go to the movies, then have dinner afterwards; 800-881-MEET, 305-755-4920 in Broward County, or 407 784-8861 in Brevard County.

• *Mosaic Outdoor Club of South Florida.* A national organization for Jewish singles who like the outdoors (bicycling, hiking, etc.); 305-464-5229.

• *National Single Parent Resource Center.* Support groups, individual consultations, socials, and various services in Broward and Palm Beach Counties; 407-395-5512.

• *Parents Without Partners, Inc.* Good support groups and a place to meet other single parents through dances and discussions. Educational programs for all family members. Contact the chapter in your area.

• *Parents Without Partners of Florida, Inc.* Saturday night contemporary ballroom dancing; 305-553-0832.

• *Partners for Travel.* Finds travel companions for singles and orchestrates singles tours for compatible age groups; 800-866-5565. Monthly newsletter.

• *Rubenesque.* For full-figured single women and their male admirers, as well as single women interested in meeting larger men. Call Howard at 305-832-2501.

• *Sheepskin Singles.* A social group for college graduates 40 to 55 interested in friendship and educational activities; 407-368-1324.

• *Single Search National Matchmaking Service.* Computerized and personalized matchmaking. Call 800-779-8362 for information about the chapter in your area.

• *Society of Young Jewish Professionals.* Semi-annual events and parties held in Dade, Broward, and Palm Beach

Counties; 800-829-0404 (order line).

• *South Florida Vanguard.* Jewish singles 23 to 40 network, meet, and mingle; 305-460-2220.

• *Space Coast Runners.* More than 600 members. Costs $10 for students, $15 for singles, $20 for families. Write to P.O. Box 2407, Melbourne, FL 32902, or call 407-784-3050.

• *Star Singles and Club Star.* Monthly parties and happy hours for Jewish singles 21 to 39 and 35 to 55; 800-683-STAR, or 305-921-5067. No membership fee.

• *Travel Companions.* Organizes trips, cruises, and tours for singles 40 and up. Call Susana at 407-393-6448.

• *Women's International Zionist Organization (WIZO).* Hosts intellectual, cultural, and social events offering networking opportunities for international men and women. 1600-1700 active members. 10 chapters from Kendall to Boca Raton. Call Mercedes at 305-861-8860.

• *World Yacht Club.* Unofficial motto is, "If it doesn't feel good, we won't do it." 1,100 chapters across the country. Not just for singles. $100 membership fee per year (but you don't need a yacht). For details on the chapter nearest you, call 800-45-FLOAT, or 800-569-9292.

• *Yellow Brick Road.* Dances, cruises, seminars, therapy sessions, and networking in Broward and Palm Beach Counties for singles 25 to 45 and for single seniors. Call Lorain at 407-998-9911 (beginning in January 1994).

Regional Groups & Organizations

1. Boca/Delray/Boynton Beach

• *Beach Bladers of South Florida.* In-line skate club for beginner, intermediate, and advanced skaters. Call the Skateline at 407-243-3117.

• *Boating Singles Club.* Meets regularly at The Cove in Deerfield Beach; 305-570-9372.

• *Boca Raton Road Runners.* Races, social events, and monthly newsletter. More than 300 members. Annual membership is $15 for singles, $20 for families; 407-487-0605.

• *Florida Athletic Club.* For individuals interested in track and field, racewalking, and roadrunning. $15 for annual dues and newsletter. Call Bob Fine before 8 p.m. at 407-499-3370, or write to him at 3250 Lakeview Blvd., Delray Beach, FL 33445.

• *Gold Coast Ski Club.* Show teams and tournaments. Beginners welcome. Weekly meetings at Lake Ida in Delray Beach; 407-737-9423 or 407-278-9849.

• *Northeast Focal Point Senior Center.* A singles support group and a senior singles group meet at the center, 227 N.W. Second St., Deerfield Beach. Call Donna De Fronzo at 305-480-4443.

• *Love Among the Stars.* Zodiacal mate-matching for compatible singles 20 to 40. Call Arlena at 407-488-2213.

• *Psychic Entertainment Socials.* For individuals interested in the "intuitive arts." Call Arlena at 407-488-2213.

• *Singles Discussion Group.* Sessions conducted by a Licensed Marriage and Family Therapist. Opportunities for meaningful discussions and activities. $15 per session. Call Robert Fels at 407-487-4466.

• *South County Young Republicans.* Far more men than women in this under-40s group. Happy hours, speakers, panels. Write to 102 N.E. 2nd St., Suite 191, Boca Raton, or call their voice mailbox at 305-574-6091 for a calendar of events.

• *Spanish River Church.* Sunday school class and other social events for singles; 2400 N.W. 51st St., Boca

Raton; 407-994-5000.
• *Temple L'Chaim.* Friday night service attracts many singles; 75 E. 5th Ave., Delray Beach; 407-274-6200.

2. Daytona Beach Area

• *Halifax Singles Fellowship.* Dinners, monthly meetings, card games, and miniature golf outings for singles 40 and up; 904-673-0538 or 904-677-1902. $15 annual membership fee.
• *New Directions.* Professionals 25 and up help raise funds for the American Cancer Society; 904-673-3350.
• *Super Singles.* Dances, picnics, and dinners for singles 40 and up; 904-253-4061. $20 annual fee.

3. Fort Lauderdale

• *Bringing Elite Singles Together (BEST).* House parties, dances, and other social activities for Jewish singles 25 to 45. Call Fred at 305-742-2113.
• *Bonnet House Junior Alliance.* Hosts happy hours and other fundraisers to preserve Bonnet House, an historic home. Call Susan Parker at 305-563-5393.
• *Broward Junior Chamber of Commerce (Jaycees).* Monthly socials and fundraisers for a variety of non-profit organizations; 305-791-0202.
• *Christ Church United Methodist Church.* Sunday singles worship at 9:45 a.m.; 4845 N.E. 25th Ave., Fort Lauderdale. Singles group also hosts dances and various social activities. Contact Rev. Jay Kowalski at 305-771-7300.
• *Contemporaries.* Individuals 18 to 35 sponsor fundraisers to benefit the Fort Lauderdale Museum of Art; 305-525-5500. Membership is $25 plus cost of

museum membership.

• *Coral Ridge Presbyterian Church.* Singles group meets for Sunday school, bible studies, and social events; 5555 N. Federal Hwy., Fort Lauderdale; 305-771-8840.

• *David D. Cantor Senior Center.* Ballroom dancing and other social events; 5000 Nob Hill Rd., Sunrise. Call Humberto at 305-742-2299.

• *Entourage.* Professionals 30 to 80 who share a love and commitment to the performing arts; 305-522-5334.

• *Intellectual Snobs Club.* An unpretentious group that meets for open discussions about various topics. All ages welcome. Write to Arnie Perlsteinat P.O. 4801, S. University Dr., 2nd Floor, Ft. Lauderdale, FL 33328, or call 305-680-3582.

• *New River Rollers.* Huge group of beginner, intermediate, and advanced skaters. Group meeting the second Wednesday of every month. Call the Skateline, 305-537-9418 or 305-527-1062.

• *Powerboat Singles Club.* Powerboat and yacht owners meet monthly for trips to the islands, picnics, fishing contests, beach parties, and socials; 305-426-1106.

• *South Broward Wheelers.* This 400-member club sponsors weekend rides throughout the tri-county area. All riding levels and all ages welcome. Call Shari Bernhard at 305-370-4804.

• *United Singles.* Light-hearted rap sessions every Friday at 8 p.m. for singles 30 to 55. Group meets in Sunrise; 305-742-2113.

4. Gainesville

• *Gainesville Professional Singles Supper Club.* Call 904-338-9905 or 904-372-1981 for information.

• *Group Solo/Gainesville's Jewish Singles.* Contact the B'nai Israel Congregation Synagogue at 904-376-1508.

• *Keystone Heights Singles Club.* Dances and dinners; 904-473-3738.
• *Sierra Club.* Send for information: 3109 N.W. 35th Terrace, Gainesville, FL 32605.
• *Trinity Singles.* Sports, discussions, and barbecues; 904-376-6615. Or send for information: 3536 N.W. 8th Ave., Gainesville, FL 32605.
• *Wanna Dance Club.* Ballroom dancing. Contact Ralph at 904-374-8315.

5. Jacksonville

• *Jewish Community Alliance/Young Jewish Singles.* Networking for singles 21 to 35; 904-730-2100.
• *Trailblazers.* Outdoor activities and social events for singles of all ages; 904-249-3058.
• *Upbeat.* Sponsored by Volunteer Jacksonville, Inc. A singles, adult volunteer group that works on more than 50 projects a year — everything from throwing holiday parties for the elderly to planting trees. Call 904-398-7777 for information.

6. The Keys/Key West

• *Christian Singles.* Group meets at the Vineyard Christian Center on 53rd St. in Marathon Key; 305-872-3404.
• *Key West Movie/Discussion Group.* Call 305-296-7535.

7. Miami/South Beach

• *City Park Recreation Center*. Texas Two-Step and Latin American Ballroom dance classes; 305-458-2936.

• *First Wednesday Group.* An informal group of mostly single professionals 30 to 50 who get together on the first Wednesday of every month for networking and social activities. Call Ben at 305-885-8523.

• *Film Society of Miami.* Produces the Miami Film Festival in February and offers screenings, seminars, and parties for film lovers; 305-377-3456. Annual memberships start at $75. All ages welcome.

• *Miami Beach Rowing Club.* Beginner and intermediate rowing classes. Not just for singles. Meets at the Ronald W. Shane Watersports Center, 6500 Indian Creek Dr., Miami Beach; 305-864-6365.

• *Miami Beach Senior Center.* Trips, cruises, painting and dance classes, cultural activities, and social events for seniors. Call Lee Klein at 305-673-6060.

• *Miami Lakes Junior Chamber of Commerce (Jaycees).* Leadership training, community service, and social events. Call Karen at 305-822-0057 for information.

• *Positive Strokes of Miami.* Tennis and social club for singles. Round-robin mixed doubles matches Monday at 7:30 p.m. on the clay courts at Salvatore Park, 1120 Andalusia Ave., Coral Gables.; 305-382-3903.

• *Team of Enthusiastic Supporters (TOES).* Organizes wine tasting parties and other fundraisers to support the Miami City Ballet. A majority of its members are single. Call 305-532-4880 for information. $35 annual membership fee.

• *Vegetarian Singles.* Yoga classes, dinners, and parties. Leave your telephone number and address on the answering machine at 305-949-0950.

8. Naples/Fort Myers

• *Fort Myers Senior Program.* The Garden Council

and Activity Center offers quilting, ballroom and line dancing, and other activities; 813-332-1288.

• *Professionals Organized for Leadership and Opportunity (POLO).* A Naples social club that meets for business networking, fundraising, and community service projects. Hosts everything from happy hours to ski/scuba/snorkel trips for members, who are mostly singles 25 to 45. Call the hotline at 813-649-5425 or, for more information, call Amy at 813-261-1040.

• *Rotaract Club of Naples.* A community-service-oriented social group for young professionals 18 to 32; 813-434-5168.

9. Orlando/Winter Park

• *Belles and Beaus.* Singles 50 and up who like ballroom dancing. Call Peggy at 407-423-5890, or Lorainne at 407-277-4265.

• *Heart of Florida Single Civitan Club.* Hands-on work with various charity organizations. Meetings held on the second Thursday of every month. Call Ruth at 407-896-7201 for information.

• *Jewish Community Center of Central Florida.* Many activities for singles. Call Deborah at 407-679-1973 for information.

• *Orlando Singles Square and Round Dance.* Previous experience required; lessons available. Call Beverly at 407-877-8677.

• *Outdoors and Active.* Offers recreational, cultural, and social activites for singles 21 to 50; 407-263-8300. Over 1,000 members. $20 membership fee.

• *Single Christians United.* Singles church services and other activities. Call Nancy at 407-849-6080.

• *Tall Club of Central Florida.* Social activites

for men over 6'2" and women over 5'10". Call 407-898-3091 for information.

10. Palm Beach/West Palm Beach

• *Bladerunners Skate Club.* Meets Sunday mornings at 10 a.m. in West Palm Beach. Novice and intermediate skaters welcome. Lessons and skate rentals available. Call Tracy at 407-689-5747 (ext. 349).

• *Extreme Team Skate Club.* Recreational and freestyle in-line skating. Meets at 7 p.m. every Sunday at Roxy's on Clematis St. in West Palm Beach. Rentals and free instruction. Call 407-641-1144.

• *Jewish Sociable Singles.* Socials for singles 60 and up; 407-687-7593.

• *Palm Beach Pack and Paddle Club.* Year-round hiking and canoeing trips. Over 300 members. Meetings at 7:30 p.m. on the second Monday of every month at the Okeeheelee Park Nature Center, 7715 Forest Hill Blvd., West Palm Beach. Write to P.O. Box 16041, West Palm Beach, FL 33415, or call Jim at 407-627-1943.

• *Singles Boating Club of the Palm Beaches.* Sailing, powerboating, and socials for singles 35 and up. Contact Sharon at 407-842-3693.

• *Singles Dance Club of the Palm Beaches.* Dances for singles 40 and up held on Fridays from 8:30 p.m. to midnight at 1317 Florida Mango Road, West Palm Beach. Call Barbara Van Ness at 407-793-2215. Admission $5 for members and $7 for non-members.

• *Gator Snow Ski Club.* Non-profit group (not affiliated with UF) that hosts skiing and non-skiing social and recreational activities for individuals 25 and up. Two-thirds of the 800 members are single. Call Sylvia Jamieson at 407-775-9848.

11. Panama City/Pensacola

• *East Brent Baptist Church Singles Ministry.* Monthly support groups, dinners, and seminars for singles 25 and up; 904-477-5812.
• *First Baptist Church Singles Ministry.* Bible studies and Sunday school classes for singles 25 and up; 904-785-6146.
• *Olive Baptist Church Singles Ministry.* Talent shows, barbecues, and sporting events for singles 25 and up; 904-476-1932.

12. Sarasota

• *Senior Friendship Center.* Daily dances, ceramics, bridge and pool games, etc. for single seniors. Call Dorothy at 813-955-2122.
• *Young Republicans Club.* Happy hours once a month. Some members also belong to the SRQ Bachelors' Club, a high-society-type group of young professionals who get together for many reasons — one of which is to throw great parties. For information on both groups, call John Chapman at 813-366-2806.

13. Tallahassee

• *East Hill Baptist Church Singles Ministry.* Sunday sermons targeting such singles issues as esteem-building, appreciating the single life, and moving on after divorce or death of a spouse; 904-224-9911.
• *Florida Young Democrats.* This statewide political group meets every two months in a different part of Florida. Provides an excellent opportunity to get involved in state politics as well as socialize with people who share common goals. Call 800-394-3411.

• *Leon Young Democrats.* A division of the Florida Young Democrats geared specifically toward residents of Leon County. Call Gary at 904-561-4391.
• *Saint Paul's United Methodist Church Singles Ministry.* Bi-weekly dinners and parties for singles 25 and up; 904-385-5146.
• *Tallahassee After-Five Club.* Provides monthy events and nights out for women. Call Arlene at 904-877-0234.
• *Tallahassee Bare Devils.* A nudist group that organizes a "full-moon skinny dip" and a weekend retreat once a month. Call Paul at 904-222-1886, or leave a message at 904-847-8537.

14. Tampa/St. Petersburg

• *Bachelors and Bachelorettes.* Square dancing for singles. Call Jerri at the St. Pete chapter, 813-791-1825.
• *Bay Area Ultimate Frisbee Club.* Not just for singles. Great aerobic activity. Join the team — or watch them play. Newcomers welcome. Call Jeff or Emily at 813-239-1132.
• *Beginners Learning Investment Group.* Educational investment information for singles. Call John at 813-854-1343.
• *Brandon Christian Singles.* Singles 28 to 68 meet for monthly dances at the First Presbyterian Church, 121 Carver St., Brandon. Call Bruce at 813-645-0371.
• *Cornerstone Community Church.* Hosts an adult coffee house called "The Filling Station" from 7 p.m. to 10 p.m. on the first Saturday of every month at the church, 408 E. Cayuga St. in Tampa. Call Marion Young at 813-238-0976 for information.
• *First Tampa Singles Civitan Club.* Community

service and social group for singles 40 and up. Call Anne at 813-886-0258.

• *Pinellas County Unitarian Universalist Singles.* Sunday meetings and evening socials in Clearwater. Call Shirley at 813-733-9066.

• *St. Cecelia's Interparish Singles.* Meetings and dances at the church in St. Petersburg. Call Naomi at 813-593-3505.

• *St. Petersburg Bicycle Club.* Not just for singles. Organizes weekday and weekend rides and offers opportunities to join race teams. Call Tom at 813-527-0510.

• *SAMSON Christian Singles.* "Single Adults Ministry Serving Others' Needs." Call 813-576-LIFE (813-576-5433) for information.

• *Single Purpose Ministries.* Dinners and meetings. Child care available. Call 813-577-9209, or call the activity line at 813-577-9172.

• *Single Travel and Dining Club.* Meets weekly at the Rusty Pelican Lounge, 524 Rocky Point Dr., Tampa. Call John at 813-854-1343.

• *Tampa Bay Freewheelers.* Group meets for various rides. 400 members of all ages. Call the information line at 813-933-2431.

• *Tampa Bay Windsurfers.* Seminars, races, night sails, and social activities. Call Chip or Doug at 813-546-5080.

• *Upper Pinellas Singles.* Singles 40 and up meet weekly at the First United Methodist Church of Dunedin. Call Nikki at 813-733-4139.

Bibliography

Census of Population and Housing, 1990: Public Use Microdata Samples U.S. prepared by the Bureau of the Census, Washington, D.C.

-----. ***Discover Florida.*** West Palm Beach: *The Palm Beach Post*, 1992.

-----. ***Discover the Treasure Coast.*** West Palm Beach: *The Palm Beach Post*, 1992.

-----. ***FYI, The Fact Book.*** West Palm Beach: *The Palm Beach Post*, 1994.

-----. ***The Sourcebook of County Demographics***, 1990 Census Ed.

Burns, Jim and Catherine Jordan, eds. ***The Best of Florida.*** N.Y.: Prentice Hall Travel, 1991.

Ford, Norman D. ***Florida.*** Floral Park, NY: Harian Publishing, 1983.

Jacobsen, Bruce and Rollin Riggs. ***The Rites of Spring.*** Priam Books, 1982.

Kleinberg, Howard. ***Miami.*** Miami: *Miami Daily News*, 1985.

Marth, Del and Martha Marth, eds. ***Florida Almanac.*** Gretna, LA: Pelican Publishing Co., 1993.

Morris, Allen. ***The Florida Handbook 1993-94.*** Tallahassee: The Peninsular Publishing Co., 1994.

Orlando and Central Florida Access. New York: HarperCollins Publishers, 1992.

Rowan, Thomas. ***Newcomers' Guide to Florida.*** St. Petersburg: Great Outdoors Publishing Co., 1985.

Zach, Paul. ***Florida.*** Hong Kong: APA Productions, 1982.

About the Author

Felicia Michele Haber, 28, is a freelance journalist living in South Florida. She is a graduate of the University of Florida School of Journalism and a reporter for *The Miami Herald* from 1989-1994. She is currently a freelance columnist for *The Herald*, reporting on nightlife and the singles scene in Broward County. This is her first book.